COLLEGE
ADMISSIONS
AND THE
PSYCHOLOGY
OF TALENT

CLIFF W. WING, JR.
MICHAEL A. WALLACH
Duke University

COLLEGE ADMISSIONS AND THE PSYCHOLOGY OF TALENT

HOLT, RINEHART AND WINSTON, INC.
New York   Chicago   San Francisco   Atlanta
Dallas   Montreal   Toronto   London   Sydney

PREFACE

When an institution of higher education admits some applicants and rejects others, the question arises of how these decisions are reached. That the matter is of pressing social significance hardly needs emphasis. For example, the December 20, 1969, issue of the *Saturday Review* called attention to it by blazoning on its cover, in relation to the idea of open admissions, the query, "Will Everyman Destroy the University?" One comes away from reading that issue, as one does from other discussions of the subject in the news media and in scholarly publications, with the overall impression that four basic options tend to get formulated as the alternatives among which to choose. The first of these options is that selection of applicants should take place on a meritocratic basis, and meritocratic selection is taken to mean selection in terms of intellective aptitude test scores and secondary school grades. The second option is that selection should proceed on a random basis. The third is that selection should explicitly favor disadvantaged students. And the fourth is that there should be open admissions—that no selection be exercised at all.

If access to the most academically prestigious colleges can in fact be genuinely available to everyone who seeks such access, that is obviously the most desirable solution to the college admissions problem. Achievement of such a goal, however, would require an unprecedented infusion of wealth into the nation's higher educational system. We are referring, of course, not to the admission of anyone to just *any* college, but to the admission of anyone to the very best programs of higher education that can be created. Open admissions in this latter sense—the only sense in

v

which it would be a meaningful solution to the admissions problem—is not going to take place on a broad scale, much as we would like to see that happen. It will not take place because the kind of money it would require is not going to be spent on education. Not by this society—and probably not by any society. Moreover, it is doubtful that even limitless funds could produce instant excellence in a greatly expanded number of higher educational institutions.

In the absence of complete access for everybody to the highest quality of educational resources, we find ourselves face to face with the inexorable need for selection—for admission of some fraction of the candidates who apply—on the part of those institutions that are in the greatest demand because of the quality of their educational resources. This throws us back, therefore, upon the first three options listed above, as far as customary discussions of the topic are concerned. But random selection and selection favoring disadvantaged students—the second and third options—are nonmeritocratic principles; they do not help each student fulfill himself to the maximum of his potential. The option of random selection is an attempt to escape the responsibility of developing rational solutions, themselves inevitably involving value judgments and difficult choices. Selection to favor disadvantaged students assumes that priority should be placed upon compensating students from disadvantaged backgrounds even at the risk that such compensation may deprive some talented students from advantaged backgrounds of the opportunity to acquire education of the highest quality. In other words, a disadvantaged background is given priority over merit. Thus both the second and the third options are basically unfair because instead of placing the highest value upon merit, they give preference, respectively, to mere chance and to circumstances of birth.

The voice of reason and practicality, therefore, which contends that the fairest basis for college admissions is a meritocratic one favoring students in accordance with our best estimates of their potential contribution to society, finds it relatively easy to support the first course of action in its broad outline—selection in terms of intellective aptitude test scores and academic achievement in high school. If anything, the test scores tend to receive greater attention than the grades because they are viewed as coming closer to the real indication of intelligence and hence of true merit.

While we fully concur that the colleges' selection of students should be based first and foremost upon merit, we believe that most current applications of the principle—the specific practices carried out in the name of a meritocratic solution to the problem—follow from an essentially wrong conception of the psychological nature of talent. There is a premise which the customary practices leave unexamined, and in our estimation this premise is crucial. The premise is that intellective aptitude test scores and high school grades constitute the most appropriate and valid definition of merit as far as college admissions are concerned. But what do we mean by merit? Not, surely, a student's intellective aptitude test scores per se, or his grades as such. These are presumed to be indicators of his potential for making meaningful contributions in the world. If intelligence test scores and grades tell us only about further grade-getting ability, rather than about talented attainments that directly reflect excellence or competence in real-world pursuits, then our meritocratic criterion is a paradoxical one indeed. In this present book we examine the aforementioned premise and find that it does not seem to be defensible when it comes to intellective aptitude test scores and grades within the upper ranges. Data are presented demonstrating that it is within just these ranges and upon the basis of precisely this premise that the selection processes operate which determine who receives admission to the more sought after colleges and universities. We then point out that defining merit in terms that, while not ignoring test scores and grades entirely, nevertheless seem better to approximate how talent in fact manifests itself, yields admissions practices that diverge sharply from those that currently prevail.

More specifically, our purpose is to make both empirical and interpretive contributions. Chapters 3, 5, 6, and 7 of our book present original research on what characteristics of students actually determine college admissions decisions, on why the actual admissions practices at high selectivity institutions are not appropriate in terms of the nature of talent, and on an alternative approach that is not only more appropriate in terms of the psychology of talent but also in fact is demonstrated to make a sizable difference regarding who would be accepted for admission. Chapters 1, 2, 4, and 8 explore the meaning of talent, place student characteristics that may bear upon college admissions into historical and conceptual perspective, examine the system of higher education in the United States in relation to the significance of college admissions, consider why the admissions practices at the nation's more prestigious colleges and universities are of substantial importance both at the level of the individual and at the level of the society, discuss the factors responsible for the present situation regarding admissions practices, and summarize the changes that our evidence leads us to recommend.

We are grateful to Douglas M. Knight and R. Taylor Cole, former President and former Provost, respectively, of Duke University, for their strong and sympathetic support of our work. Financial assistance relevant to some of the work described in this book was provided in part by a grant from the Richardson Foundation and in part by Duke University. Emily Chen, Lynn Clark, Philip W. Graham, and Marilyn Petersen aided us as research assistants with various aspects of the studies. Clark R. Cahow, University Registrar, supplied us with duplicates of Duke's applicant files, and William L. Brinkley, Jr., former Director of Undergraduate Admissions, was most cooperative in his willingness to include some research materials in the college application forms and in sharing with us his extensive information about Duke students. Data analyses were carried out at the Duke University Computing Laboratory, which is supported in part by a grant from the National Science Foundation. Thanks are owed Dean K. Whitla, Director of the Office of Tests at Harvard, who encouraged us to re-think and make more effective use of certain statistical techniques through his vigorous questioning of our approach. Secretarial assistance was skillfully provided by Barbara Cameron, Margaret Dellerson, Judy Edquist, and Carol Greenlaw. And finally, we are grateful to David L. Rosenhan and Lise Wallach for their perceptive comments on the manuscript.

The producing of this volume has been a truly collaborative endeavor: each of us has learned from the other in the process. From two quite different backgrounds of experience—in the first case, an applied perspective generated by the activities of college admissions, and in the second, a theoretical perspective arising from research on cognitive and social processes—we were brought together by the belief that the meshing of these perspectives might throw a brighter light on talent and its utilization by the society. In the course of moving from that belief to what is presented in this volume, the first of us has no doubt become more theoretical, and the second of us more applied, than he was before. We find it hard to distinguish individual contributions, therefore, and the order of authorship corresponds to the sequence in which our respective backgrounds are represented in the book's title.

Cliff W. Wing, Jr.
Michael A. Wallach

Durham, North Carolina
September 1970

CONTENTS

CHAPTER ONE

Student Characteristics
and the Admissions Process

Over the past 50 years there has evolved a complex, variable process by means of which secondary school graduates migrate to the nation's colleges and universities. The flight patterns of these migratory flocks range from near to far, from direct to circuitous, from prestigious institutions to community colleges. While some systematic patterns are observable, others are obscure. Most students go to colleges not far from home; but what colleges happen to be near home? And many students go far afield—some flying the airways from coast to coast in complicated, apparently unpredictable patterns. How can these wide variations be described, much less explained? If we are to win order from this seeming chaos, the migratory patterns will have to be examined in the light of two kinds of issues: differences in the students and differences in the colleges and universities.

What is our stake in learning about the admissions process—the process that puts one young person into a college around the corner, another into a university across the continent, and a third into a job that does not require a college education? First of all, we are interested in the behavior of these flocks for the sake of the knowledge itself. What are the mechanisms of flight, the tropisms affecting it? How is it all done? What kinds of individuals receive the highly advantaged treatment that admission to the best institutions confers; what kinds must go elsewhere? But this particular annual migration has implications for the nature of the entire society. The students deemed worthy of preferential access to the better colleges are by that fact being propelled more vigorously into positions of leadership in the nation, just as those who go to college at all become more influential than those who do not. To the extent that superior educational opportunities are less available to those who exhibit certain forms of talent and more available to those who exhibit other forms, the overall values, goals, and attainments of the society become more reflective of the latter than the former kinds of individuals. In sum, the practices that govern who goes where to college are too important in shaping this country's modes of talent utilization, and hence

1

in shaping the country itself, to be allowed entrenchment without examination.

Thirty years ago, 14 percent of the 18- to 21-year-old population attended college. In 1965 the comparable figure was 46 percent, and the expectation is that it will reach 55 percent by 1974. In terms of numbers of students, the total college enrollment about 30 years ago was on the order of 1.3 million; by 1965 it had reached 5.5 million; and the projection for 1974 is 8.7 million (Hoyt, 1968). As the numbers going to college have increased, there have been concomitant changes in the admissions process. In the early 1900s, the matter of who went to college was based almost entirely on the availability of financial resources or on the presence of a specific desire to enter one of the relatively few professions demanding college preparation. By contrast, today the college degree is a prerequisite for entrance not only into a greatly expanded spectrum of professions but also into most positions wherein above average economic rewards are customarily available. Viewed another way, it has become a prerequisite for most positions of trust, responsibility, or leadership in the society. Whether we like it or not, the world is becoming an increasingly complex place, and the coping skills demanded by the society will most likely continue to show a parallel increase in their degree of dependence upon higher education and upon who receives the opportunities offered by such education. So also, as we noted before, will the very nature of that society in terms of its emphases, its spirit, and the kinds of paths that it follows from among the wider range of possibilities open to it.

Given the great importance of college education in this society, therefore, it is crucial to learn how the decisions are made about who goes to what college—about the characteristics of students who are admitted to the different kinds of colleges, and about the characteristics of applicants who are turned down by various kinds of colleges. Is it all as common sense might suggest, or are we in for some surprises? Our first task—a kind of propaedeutic to the enterprise—is classification and description of the major elements that bear upon the admissions process so that the interlocking nature of these elements may be better understood. We will gain in this way the tools needed for our further discussion and our analyses of data. Classification and description constitute the necessary first step in accumulating knowledge about any kind of physical, biological, or psychosocial process—and the process of college admissions is no exception. We well realize the potential dangers of ill-fitting classifications and of typologies that fail to do justice to the facts. Whatever the pitfalls, however, a beginning must be made. In order to describe the elements that play a role in the admissions process, then, we will consider in this first chapter some characteristics of the students who apply for admission, and in the next chapter, some characteristics of the institutions that assess the students' applications.

People obviously differ from one another in multitudinous ways, from simple physical appearance to esoteric qualities of style. Among these many kinds of differences, our interest is in describing those which seem to impinge upon college admission to at least some degree. First of all, one may discern a range of characteristics that reflect the circumstances of a person's birth. These kinds of individual differences we refer to as *status characteristics*—and by this we mean what a sociologist would call matters of ascribed status or demographic attributes. The characteristics that accrue from circumstances of birth include such factors as sex, race, the parents' residence, their religious affiliation, their socioeconomic and educational attainments, the cultural and economic resources of their community, and the urban, suburban, or rural character of that community. This is not an all-inclusive list of status characteristics, but it contains the main ones. And such characteristics are the forge for shaping other distinguishing attributes that we describe with names like intelligence, further possible aptitude or ability characteristics that can be separated from intelligence, personality, interests, values, and attitudes. This latter set of traits we call *personal characteristics*.

By personal characteristics we mean those attributes, inferred from a person's behavior, that are presumed to function as signs of the potential for manifesting intrinsically valued forms of conduct or intrinsically valued products. Unlike status characteristics, personal characteristics cannot be defined without reference to a person's behavior. Such concepts as intelligence or attitudes are ways of summarizing behavior that are viewed as offering a prognosis on how likely the person is to show types of conduct or to achieve products that are considered to possess intrinsic worth. In this category we group those behaviorally inferred attributes which, while not viewed as meritorious in their own right, are thought to indicate the potential for meritorious accomplishments on the individual's part. Thus, for example, interest in fine arts is viewed as a prerequisite to artistic achievement, and a humanitarian attitude is considered as a sign of the potential for humanitarian deeds. So also, answering more questions correctly on an intelligence test and therefore earning a higher IQ score than somebody else is not per se valuable because one isn't really interested in the answers to these particular questions. Rather, one is interested in the assumed promise that the ability to answer more of these questions correctly is a valid indication that the bearer of the higher test score possesses a greater likelihood of demonstrating accomplishments that are in fact valued in their own right by the society— such as carrying out a worthwhile scientific project or writing a story that wins critical acclaim.

Out of the matrix provided by status characteristics and personal characteristics there emerges a third category of individual differences which we call *accomplishment characteristics*. This category refers to kinds of behavior and products of behavior that are valued in their own right. They are not viewed as promissory notes for something else, but to at least some degree as ends in themselves. Based upon his own set of status characteristics and his own array of personal characteristics, an individual performs in ways and creates products that are viewed by his environment as possessing greater or lesser intrinsic worth. He takes piano lessons and gives a recital that wins high praise. He carries out on his own a biology project that wins a national award. He tries unsuccessfully for a 4-H Club award for the potato crop he raised. He paints pictures that gain attention in an art exhibition that is sent around the state. He is elected student body president. He gets a rejection slip from a magazine. He plays the lead role in a dramatic performance and gains praise for his performance. He makes the all-state football team. He goes to school and makes grades reflecting his achievement in various subjects. Short of an exhaustive delineation of the actual criteria for defining intrinsic worth of performances and products—a formidable task, indeed, as any philosopher will assure us—environmental judgments of these kinds seem to offer the best clues as to quality level that are available in practice.

To group academic achievement—the matter we just mentioned—as an accomplishment characteristic along with the other examples given requires additional comment. For all the other cases, such as writing something that is or is not considered worthy of publication, or painting a picture that is or is not deemed worthy of public exhibition, or winning or failing to win critical acclaim for acting ability, we are describing behavior and outcomes of behavior that tend to be viewed as possessing greater or lesser value in themselves. The situation for academic achievement is different. While the society often talks as if school grades are an end in themselves, it really intends school to function as a practice environment permitting development and assessment of competencies to deal with the outside world. The use of achievement terminology for referring to academic prowess—terminology implying that such prowess possesses intrinsic worth—thus really is misleading. By and large, the value of a higher grade average actually rests in its presumed ability to indicate a greater likelihood of making meaningful contributions to the real-life environment—that is, the world beyond the classroom. Intrinsic worth for grades would hold only in those cases where they happen to reflect the making of an innovative or integrative academic contribution—such as the writing of a genuinely creative term paper—not for those cases where they reflect the feeding back of material that is all too familiar to the teacher. It is obviously the latter type of work that constitutes the lion's share of what academic achievement for most students is about. Grades of A rather than B or C in science courses, for example, are presumed to reflect a greater potential for becoming a good scientist. Do they in fact have this meaning? We shall return to this question later in the chapter. In sum, then, academic achievement tends to straddle the distinction we have drawn between accomplishment characteristics and personal characteristics—and, if anything, to be closer to the latter than to the former category as far as its real meaning is concerned. We will leave academic achievement grouped as an accomplishment characteristic, however, because the culture has attached achievement terminology to the business of earning academic grades and we don't want to do that much violence to a cultural label.

The issue just raised is far from an exercise in classification. It brings into focus the crucial question of what in fact *ought* to be considered accomplishment characteristics—that is, characteristics viewed as possessing intrinsic merit. Education tends to treat grade point average as if it were an accomplishment characteristic, whereas for the most part it really is a personal characteristic, a promissory note for post-schooling attainments. Of all the accomplishment characteristics that we passed in review as examples, the only one whose membership in the category can be seriously questioned is academic achievement. But how much attention does the educational system in fact pay to the other kinds of accomplishment characteristics that we considered—the ones manifested outside of the academic routine? It would be ironic indeed if relatively incontrovertible accomplishment characteristics—acts and products of relatively clear intrinsic worth—receive less attention than academic achievement, which for the most part matters not in itself but only if it functions as a valid indicator of attainments beyond the school environment.

We have been speaking about ways in which people differ from one another that seem to affect in at least some degree an applicant's prospects for college admission. Having grouped these kinds of differences into status, personal, and accomplishment characteristics, and having analyzed what we mean by these categories, we will now consider what can be said on the basis of overall impressions and of already available information as to how these characteristics bear upon college-going opportunities and what these characteristics mean for one another.

Status Characteristics

Let us examine status characteristics once again. Students whose parents went to college, or whose parents work in occupations suggesting college backgrounds, are much more likely to seek a college education themselves than are their contemporaries whose parents did not go to college (Tyler, 1965). Furthermore, students usually have a better chance of admission to a parent's alma mater than to a college with which the family has had no previous association—a fact evident from the routine figures issued by colleges comparing the percentage of alumni children accepted with the percentage of applicants with no alumni connection accepted. An applicant's sex controls his admissability to a non-coeducational college. The state or region where a high school student resides may have a very important effect on his chances for admission to college. Some states routinely provide higher education opportunities for all high school graduates who are residents, while these same states maintain entirely different and far more stringent standards for students from out of state. Residence also affects a student's chances for entrance into institutions that seek to assemble a student body geographically representative of the entire country. A student applying to such a college may be one of 500 applicants residing in a state from which 50 will be selected —thus giving him odds of one in ten—or one of 100 applicants residing in a state from which 33 will be chosen—thus giving him odds of one in three. Also, if the particular community or school from which the student comes is one that traditionally sends a majority of its high school graduates on to college, the facilities available for college counseling and, as a consequence, the chances for college placement are greater.

Turning next to race, the application pattern for college entrance found among blacks is undergoing rapid change. Until the late 1960s, blacks were severely under-represented in the college-going population as a whole and, in particular, at what were predominantly white institutions, whether by policy or de facto. Today, however, in an effort to obtain a larger proportion of nonwhites—especially of blacks—for their student bodies, many colleges have mounted intensive campaigns to attract these particular applicants. As a result, the status of being black now actually works as an enormous asset—at least for applicants to certain colleges. On the other hand, a black skin also can carry with it the opposing status force of a culturally disadvantaged background which fails to orient the student toward college-going as a goal. The upshot is that these two status characteristics—being black and having, presumably, a background of cultural deprivation—tend to play against one another in affecting college applications from black students.

As a final point in our review of the impact of status characteristics, note that socioeconomic standing and residence in rural areas also are factors that have been undergoing recent changes regarding the manner in which they affect candidates' chances of college admission. Many colleges search out and make special efforts to enroll students from lower socioeconomic groups and from rural areas, but these attributes interact with—and frequently seem to be overwhelmed by—the impact of other characteristics of the college applicant. As a result, we cannot conclude that being poor and growing up on a farm give the candidate an advantage. Consider two students who are equally underprivileged. The first, with substantial but not spectacular academic credentials, may have as his only affordable avenue the local community college and continue living at home. The second, in the same socioeconomic position but with an outstanding academic pedigree may be sought after and offered large inducements to attend several colleges in various parts of the country.

Personal Characteristics

While status characteristics of students have important effects upon whether and upon where they go to college, it is fair to assert that personal characteristics usually take precedence over status characteristics in the case of colleges that differentiate between the relative desirability of their candidates. Therefore, though state residency and a high school diploma are all that may be needed for admission to one college (regardless of the personal characteristics of the candidate), such characteristics will play a critical role at more selective institutions. At these latter kind, statements in their college bulletins usually set forth the personal characteristics desired of candidates.

What do we find when we open the pages of such bulletins? While the personal characteristics that are mentioned as desiderata may include aspects of students' values, attitudes, character, interests, and personality, the single factor most consistently desired is the academic aptitude shown by tests of general intelligence. For all practical purposes, the concepts of academic aptitude and general intelligence mean the same thing, since both typically refer to a student's level of skill in working with verbal and numerical symbols in various kinds of tasks.

The history of intelligence testing began in the early part of the twentieth century when it was demonstrated that scores on intelligence tests are related to grades earned in school. Documentation of the linkage between intelligence and academic achievement is available throughout the various educational levels (see, for example, Fishman, 1962; Tyler, 1965; Wallach and Kogan, 1965; Wallach and Wing, 1969). Because of the extensive evidence supporting this linkage, colleges believe they possess a sound rationale for placing reliance upon the intelligence assessments as admissions criteria. They can point to demonstrations that academic success in a college curriculum—whether measured in terms of grade point average or likelihood of graduating—is pervasively related to preadmissions scores on intelligence tests, so they view their ground as firm indeed for utilizing the latter as a screening device for candidates.

Tests of general intelligence are administered not only by colleges, when they are assessing applicants for admission, but by high schools as well. The latter use these test results as a help in providing counseling, guidance, and placement services to their students: streaming them within the high school into what are presumed to be "faster" and "slower" groups, for example; advising them about their chances of success in seeking to undertake various lines of occupational preparation; and steering them toward making applications to colleges which are likely to accept candidates within the relevant intellective test score range. Most high school students are apt to know something about their own intelligence test score levels, since use of such tests in secondary schools is so widespread. We even find Goslin citing (1967) their use, as one among several common applications of intelligence tests by high school principals, ". . . as a basis for providing the pupil with information about his abilities" (p. 15). We can expect that the students as well as their advisors will take account of the potential applicant's level of tested intelligence in formulating college plans. As a consequence Davis (1966) was able to find that those receiving recognition in the National Merit Scholarship Competition—a high intelligence group of students—tend to cluster at a relatively small number of colleges, and it is known that such students tend strongly to be accepted wherever they apply. Also, applicants to different kinds of colleges usually come from different parts of the SAT score distribution (College Entrance Examination Board, 1965). In short, pre-selection along intelligence lines takes place in college attendance. Students tend to choose collegiate institutions in accordance with a reading of their own intellective aptitude as compared with the intellective ability of students already in attendance at the colleges. The result is a congregation of certain kinds of students—defined in terms of intelligence tests—at certain colleges, and a tendency toward perpetuating the types of linkages between students and colleges that are thereby worked out.

It is not only the linkage between intelligence measures and academic achievement that provides the basis for tying intelligence level into the admissions process. Emphasis upon intelligence also is congruent with the meritocratic values of the culture. Each individual, after all, produces his own score on a test that has been designed to minimize the degree to which possession of particular status characteristics will enhance his performance. Normative comparisons concerning the test are available on a nationwide basis, so that a maximally broad frame of reference can be adopted from which to view how any particular student stands up. The consequence is a score that is relatively easy to interpret and is relatively free from contamination by unequal opportunities regarding school and family background—at least to the extent that high school students who have taken four years of Latin or four years of mathematics are deprived of an automatic advantage over those who have not. And, the score gives the decision-maker something other than status characteristics to consider. Measures of intelligence introduced into the selection process over the past 25 years have without a doubt served to broaden college opportunities for the population, leading therefore to an evident democratization of higher education. No longer is it the case that attendance at a selective college will be dependent almost entirely upon the status-determined accidents of having enrolled in particular preparatory schools, having followed a narrowly prescribed set of college preparatory courses, or having come from the kind of family that renders the obtaining of the "right" sort of college preparatory background a foregone conclusion.

Given the apparent virtues of intelligence tests that have the power to predict grades while at the same time reflecting the meritocratic value of tapping ability rather than status, it follows that the educational world values the student who makes a high test score. The secondary school student with a high intelligence test score will be vigorously pursued by college recruiters. Colleges seem in fact to rank order themselves informally in terms of the average intellective ability level of their students, thus making acquisition of more high test scorers a source of institutional prestige. The message that a college puts forth to its institutional competitors seems to be something like, "We, too, have bright students," or "We have more National Merit finalists than you do." It follows that students with high test scores—say, scores falling within the top two or three percent of the national distribution for students who take the test—learn early not only that college is available to them but also that they will be able to choose among a variety of colleges. In effect, they find themselves, relatively speaking, in a seller's market, receiving in fact letters of invitation from many colleges. On the other hand, students with test scores that are more modest although still falling well within a range for which going-to-college represents an appropriate activity—say, scores located within the top 50 percent of the national norm for the students who took the test—will more likely be left to their own devices: they will have to seek out college opportunities for themselves, or take what is available, rather than be sought after by colleges.

With the kind of role that intelligence level seems to play with regard to admissions, the question of how well tested intelligence serves to indicate a student's likelihood of manifesting attainments that are intrinsically valuable in their own right clearly is very important. We know that intellective aptitude predicts grades; but we have also seen that while grades are viewed as intrinsically meritorious, for the most part their significance rests upon their import for real-life accomplishments. Since intellective level and academic achievement are closely related, we will deal simultaneously later in this chapter with the matter of relationships between each of them and life-defined accomplishments.

Intelligence certainly is not the only personal characteristic that impinges upon college entrance. Personality assessment of one form or another also tends to have some role in the admissions process. As a personal characteristic or as a subclass of such characteristics, the term "personality" obviously covers a rather amorphous range of dispositions. Included here would be such matters as a student's presumed degree of motivation for academic achievement and the presumed degree of tranquility or storminess that characterizes his relationships with other people. The reasoning that most easily brings personality considerations into the admissions picture is that if an insufficient drive for achievement is present, then grade level will suffer—and grade level functions here in an institution's scheme of things as an intrinsic value. So also, it would be reasoned that if a student's emotional difficulties are too intense he is less likely to earn respectable grades or to graduate, and may even contaminate the collegiate atmosphere in such a manner as to reduce the likelihood of other students succeeding academically. Apart from the more patent instances of very low achievement motivation or strong emotional disturbance, however, personality assessments lack a discernible relationship with academic achievement. Conventional psychological instruments for the measurement of aspects of personality have little demonstrable meaning for the prediction of academic success in college (Stein, 1963). The consequence is that the serious use of personality assessments in admissions work would really boil down to taking a position on the issue of what particular personality types are more valuable and what types less so, in the sense not of predicted grade point average but of the likelihood that the student will go on to do something meaningful after school. While, ironically, the latter is precisely what should constitute the major selection basis, since excellence in life pursuits clearly is the ultimate concern of the selection process, personality concepts are sufficiently elusive in themselves, and in the attempt to move from conceptual to measurement levels, that there is little by way of usable knowledge concerning such matters. Perhaps especially because colleges tend to preconceive that because personality assessments are unrelated to grades they will be unrelated to real-life accomplishments, it is our impression that such assessments play only a minor role in college admissions.

Nevertheless, there undoubtedly is a small group of colleges that try to make systematic use of personality assessments for admissions purposes—colleges wherein the competition for admission is the keenest. The methods by which such colleges attempt to carry out personality assessments usually are other than those through standard psychological instruments, for these techniques, as already noted, have borne little fruit in terms of relationships with criteria that would serve to legitimize their use. The methods which do tend to be used at these institutions can be grouped roughly into four general categories—although these definitely are not fully exhaustive of the kinds of evaluations that are carried out: (1) requests on application forms for samples of the applicant's writing ability; (2) requests for biographical histories to be written by the applicant; (3) interviews with the applicant conducted by members of the admissions staff or by alumni representatives who assist them; and (4) confidential evaluations requested from secondary school personnel or from other references concerning the applicant's life style, his typical ways of handling new situations, and his customary reactions to the high school environment.

Colleges that genuinely rely in some degree on such information as the above do not, in our estimation, use this material for ordering individuals along a dimension, as is the practice with scores on intelligence tests. Rather than trying to score the degree to which a particular trait is possessed by a student, the personality assessments are used to form rough impressions on the basis of which the students can be grouped into types. The result may be as rough as attempting to distinguish between "good guys" and "bad guys" or between "doers" and "grinds." On the other hand, the typology may be somewhat more refined—as when one student is classified as "likely to have a high grade point average without making any contribution to other aspects of the college environment," a second as "likely to be both an academic achiever and an innovative contributor outside the classroom," and a third as "capable of satisfactory academic performance, but his chief promise is in athletics"—or in some other line of extracurricular endeavor that may be of value to the college.

Some institutions have attempted to infer from personality assessments how the student will react to the pressures that await him if he enters the college environment in question. Thus Glimp (1967) and Whitla (1968), both of Harvard, have been concerned about the effects upon Harvard students of being made to feel academically average in a highly competitive academic environment where grades are the pervasive yardstick used by students for arriving at judgments of their own worth. Students who were academically superior at the secondary school level— the norm for Harvard admittees—will find it a new experience to be located in the middle or at the bottom of their class at college. Yet, of necessity, that is where most will end up. Attempts are made in the admissions process, therefore, to assess the applicant's ability to adjust to being average or undistinguished as far as grades are concerned, while retaining a feeling of self-confidence and attaining success in other areas of endeavor.

Personality assessments therefore chiefly affect the mobility of high school graduates who hope to move on into colleges that are quite high in their selectivity. The chances for acceptance of such applicants may be enhanced or curtailed in part on the basis of personality considerations that we have described. Students' interests regarding career and vocational choices also affect college acceptance in ways which—as in the case of intelligence—again focus in two directions. On the one hand, interest patterns influence the colleges to which a student will seek admission; on the other, these patterns influence which students will seem more desirable to a college. Examples of the former causal sequence are high school graduates who already have definite vocational interests. These students often limit their applications to institutions that have a well-formulated curriculum in the area of their particular interest. Colleges, on the other hand, sometimes recruit and admit students differentially as a function of their expressed interest in one or another type of curricular offering. At some institutions, for example, students with vocational interests in a particular branch of the fine arts may have favorable action taken upon their applications in cases where, had they made no specific expression regarding a career interest and indicated instead that they simply were interested in liberal arts, they would have been turned down. Institutional practices of this kind stem from a desire to sustain or increase student populations in various undergraduate programs. Hence a strongly expressed interest in what happens to be an underpopulated program may be the deciding factor that wins a student an admissions ticket. Even within the liberal arts division, a college may decide to over-admit to, say, science programs because the dropout rate from such programs at the end of the freshman year is high and the college wishes to maintain a given ratio of science majors to other majors during the junior and senior years.

Assessment of students' interests for purposes of college admissions rests principally upon what the students put down on their application forms. Conventional psychological measures of vocational and career interests have not been widely used by colleges—once again for the reason that such indicators have not yielded accurate forecasts of academic success. These measures are, however, sometimes used in high school counseling and guidance programs in order to help students define their preferences. To the extent that the results of these counselor-administered tests then enter into the student's decision-making process, they end up playing a part in the ultimate match between student and institution. But generally, information regarding students' interest patterns for college admissions purposes remains relatively informal.

The subclass of student personal characteristics that can be termed values or value systems blends, of course, with the matters of interests and interest patterns just described. When interests become sufficiently generic or broad, we refer to them as values or attitudes. Like interests, values also affect the migratory pattern by which students enroll in colleges. Once again the causal process works both ways. A student may place high value on a liberal arts education, or he may place little value on any particular kind of undergraduate program and simply be seeking higher education of some kind. Another student may place no importance whatever on higher education. Some students will put a premium on pursuits of an abstract, nonapplied nature, while others will be drawn toward pursuits that have apparent immediate applicability. Other students will put relationships with their fellow men as a foremost consideration in their lives, and still others will be strongly moved by the esthetic effect of what impinges on their sense organs. Such value differences obviously influence applications to college and to what kinds of institutions. If higher education is sought, the program desired may range from technological pursuits at the local junior college to the study of Greek mythology in the classics department of a university. Colleges, too, will differentially seek students that exemplify different value orientations, as a function of how each particular institution reads its own educational mandate.

Psychological instruments for assessing students' values rarely receive direct use in the admissions process. Rather, most colleges attempt to deduce something about the values of their applicants by seeking information concerning such matters as the highest degree to which they aspire—whether, for example, it is a Bachelor's degree, a Master's degree, a Ph.D., or a professional degree—and the kind of career choice to which they seem oriented. On the other hand, research by Heist (1968) has utilized value assessments of a more direct nature in order to explore relationships between the values held by students who are on the campus and the ways in which they come to terms with college life.

Accomplishment Characteristics

From personal characteristics we move now to the third broad grouping—accomplishment characteristics. Recalling our earlier explication of this category, we refer here to behaviors and the results of behavior that stand at least to some extent as ends in themselves. A poem or short story receives greater or lesser acclaim as an esthetic product. The same fate awaits a piece of sculpture. A scientific project yields a contribution to a field of knowledge. Attempts at political leadership are more or less successful at winning general recognition as acts of statesmanly skill. An article is written that helps to illuminate our understanding of a particular historical era. A performance on the violin or of a particular part in a play strikes us as very impressive. It is such attainments as these that define, of course, what the possession of competencies in actual life settings is all about. Accomplishments of these kinds are exhibited already in some degree, however, by the time a student is involved in what are called "extracurricular" activities during the high school years. Thus, one student will write a play that is performed and well received. Another will have several stories published in a nationally circulated magazine. A third will find some rare form of vegetation in the country and make some further observations concerning it that turn out to be of interest to botanists. On the other hand, a student may write a play that loses out in a contest for performance; another student will try to write a few scenes of a play and then give up. Still another will write stories that are published in the school literary magazine but are not accepted by a national magazine. And yet another will think about writing a story but never get around to it. The kinds of performances and products that have been illustrated possess intrinsic worth—they are valuable in their own right to a greater or lesser degree. It is this feature which distinguishes them from personal characteristics, where relevance to college admission depends upon assuming that what has been learned about the student signifies something about what we can expect him to do in terms of accomplishments.

We begin our consideration of accomplishment characteristics not with what has just been described, however, but with a type of accomplishment that only dubiously fulfills our definitional requirement: academic achievement. While the society tends to treat academic achievement as an end in itself, thus leading to our classifying it as an accomplishment characteristic, the real significance of such achievement depends on how valid it is as a sign that not just the school's but also the world's standards for meritorious attainments will be met. If academic achievement tells us nothing about what to expect from a person as soon as he steps outside of school, it obviously tells us little that we want to know. Of all the accomplishment characteristics that are available to potential view in high school students, however, it is academic achievement—the transcript of courses and grades—that is most influential in the college admissions process.

The secondary school grade record does provide the colleges with an index of how each applicant interacts with an environment which in many respects is quite similar to the one he will encounter in college. Since the environments are similar, the transcript of secondary school marks, whether stated in terms of grade point average or rank in class, is usually the best single predictor of freshman college grades. The positive relationship between high school grade point average and college grade point average provides the colleges with a rationale for using the former in making admissions decisions. Similarly, the link between intelligence test scores and college grades provides a comparable rationale for letting the tested intelligence level of applicants influence admissions decisions. So far as the relationship between academic achievement in general and level of accomplishment in real-life settings has not been ascertained, the type of reasoning just described begs the question. In choosing applicants for college admission in such a way as to maximize the college grade point average of the student body our interest depends—or should depend—on knowing that we are thereby improving the likelihood that the students in question will display meaningful real-life accomplishments.

Accepting the fact that intelligence test scores and high school grades both predict college grades with substantial degrees of accuracy, it is not surprising to find that level of tested intelligence and secondary school grades are highly interrelated. Because this interrelationship is quite stable around the country, colleges and universities frequently look at the joint bearing of their students' intelligence test scores and secondary school academic achievements upon grade level in college—drawing up an equation in which the relative weights assigned to tested intelligence and to secondary school grade achievement are set in such a manner as to maximize the predictability of grade point average in college. Usually, predictions of college grades based upon some combination of intelligence level and secondary school grade record are more accurate than those obtained from high school grades or intelligence test scores alone. Which combination works best?

It is risky to attempt a specific answer to this question, because the relative weights for high school marks and for intelligence test scores that would maximize the predictability of college grades vary considerably from institution to institution, from one curriculum to another within an institution, and over time for all institutions. But a general answer can be offered. Maximum predictability can be obtained when the intellective test scores are weighted less than one-half and the high school record is weighted more than one-half in the prediction equation—that is, in the formula predicting college grades as a function of test scores and secondary school grades. While this contention is based on our overall impression of the results obtained from various prediction studies, it is also supported by recent empirical evidence gathered by Hoyt (1968). From the sampling of colleges evaluated, Hoyt found that the best-weight equations for predicting college grades ranged from weighting intelligence test scores and high school grade level in the ratio of 1 to 0.7, to weighting test scores and grade level in the ratio of 1 to 3.2, with a median ratio of 1 to 1.2. That high school grades are more significant than tested intelligence for predicting college grades is obvious, of course, from the aforementioned fact that academic achievement in high school and college constitute reactions to similar environments.

Over the last 20 years many institutions have used the results of these prediction studies to decide which applicants should be admitted. Realizing that intelligence level tests and high school grades both predict attainable college grades and that a particular weighted combination of the two makes for better predictions than either alone, a college will weight its applicants' scores in the same way as it does those of its on-campus students and thus decide whom to accept and whom to reject. Apart from weighting subtleties, however, the basic point is that account is taken both of tested intelligence and of high school academic achievement, with higher levels of one viewed as compensating in some degree for lower levels of the other. Consequently an applicant's access to college often is cast simultaneously in terms both of intelligence level and high school record. For example, high tested intelligence may compensate for lack of distinguished grade achievement in high school as far as getting into a particular college is concerned, while a distinguished grade record may analogously compensate for lower levels of tested intellective ability. So too, a student who ranks in the top ten percent of his high school class and who shows average tested intelligence might be accepted by a college which would reject a student of the same intellective ability level who ranked in the middle of his class. And again, a student of high tested intelligence and average grades might be admitted to a college that would turn down a student with the same academic record but a lower intellective ability score.

In sum, tested intelligence and secondary school achievement are combined into an essentially unidimensional index of an applicant's desirability. Applicants who meet these terms have an easier time as far as college entrance is concerned. Students who have earned high grades and intelligence test scores can choose from a considerably wider range of colleges than can those whose grades and test scores are more modest. Students who do relatively well on one type of assessment and less well on the other, in turn, fall between the other two groups regarding college opportunities. Secondary school grades and intelligence test scores—themselves closely related—exercise a pervasive influence over the migration pattern from high school to college.

Intelligence test scores, however, and most of the personal information that goes into a student's record of academic achievement cannot be viewed as ends in themselves—although the accomplishment terminology with which our society refers to academic grades makes this confusing. Intelligence tests are measures of academic aptitude—the ability to do well in school. What then, in relation to accomplishments outside of school, is the evidence for rating students on their presumed worthiness by considering their tested intelligence and their grade point averages? In other words, how well grounded is the implicit assumption behind the use of intelligence tests and grades for making merit distinctions? Does this information have the power to indicate which applicants are likely to exhibit noteworthy attainments in their real-life pursuits?

The awareness has been gradually dawning that this power may be somewhat illusory in the upper part of the range for academic skills. About a decade ago McClelland (1958) called attention to this point by suggesting that there is a serious lack of conformity between performance in school and performance in life. He raised the issue by referring to our general experience of two types of students—those who appeared relatively unimpressive in their school setting but who went on to carry out significant work in the outside world, and those who looked extremely impressive in terms of academic aptitude and achievement but who never fulfilled their apparent promise. McClelland gave the former type the label of "late bloomers," the latter, that of "morning glories." Their existence, he pointed out, flies in the face of what he recognized to be the fundamental assumption made by scientists and laymen alike concerning the nature of talent: namely, that intelligence ". . . is linearly associated with success both in school and in life. . ." (McClelland, 1958, p. 14). He expressed the belief that ". . . some college admission requirements, both on aptitude test scores and secondary school records, are so strict that it is doubtful whether some of our leading citizens could get into these schools or colleges now." (p. 9.) From these considerations he drew the following conclusion: "It is this lack of fit between school and life—the constant reminder of the 'late bloomers' and the 'morning glories'—that forces us, perhaps more than any other single factor, to scrutinize the whole problem of talent." (pp. 9–10.)

Just to be able to cite from one's general experience instances of late bloomers and morning glories, however, does not provide a sufficient basis for mounting a critique of how the society defines the meaning of talent. These instances can, after all, be viewed simply as the exceptions that prove the rule. If their incidence were sufficiently low, they would constitute nothing more than the inevitable degree of error that one encounters when applying any systematic means of talent assessment. Supporters of heavy dependence on intelligence testing and grades for defining human excellence would argue that one must make selections for preferential treatment in *some* way, after all, and the way which they recommend works out more soundly in practice than any other way. Clearly, then, we need to move beyond citation of particular cases of late bloomers and morning glories and offer systematic evidence that permits us to assess, across the upper part of the academic skills range, the usefulness of intelligence and grade-level information to predict attainment in real-life occupational situations. Only recently systematic evidence of this kind appeared. Let us consider in detail some illustrative findings concerning occupational excellence, and then sum up where this kind of consideration leads. Plainly, however, we are concerned with only the upper part of the range for academic skills. We do not doubt that intelligence and grade information can be appropriately used for eliminating candidates whose level of academic competence is too weak to make successful completion of a given college's curriculum a likely outcome. It is with choices among candidates above such a level that we are concerned.

As an example of such research, we point to a study by Harmon (1963). Not only does this study illustrate the typical outcome of the question, but it shows how deeply ingrained is the assumption that intelligence and school grades *must* be prognostic of one's accomplishment level in post-college occupations. Harmon's sample consisted of 347 physical scientists and 157 biological scientists, most of whom had earned Ph.D.'s. These were grouped into different experience categories depending on how many subsequent years had been spent in work situations. Because somewhat different considerations applied in assessing the level of contribution within the two scientific domains in question, separate groupings were made not only for amount of experience but also for the fields of physical and biological sciences. The scientists in the study were identified on the basis of their having applied earlier in their careers for graduate school fellowship support from the National Science Foundation—whether the fellowships were awarded or not. In the case of each person in the study, various intelligence and academic achievement indicators were considered: verbal and quantitative aptitude test scores, results from an advanced scholastic achievement test in their main field of interest, and undergraduate grade point average for science courses. How, in turn, was level of attainment in one's professional work defined?

Three or more independent raters, themselves scientists who in most instances currently were members of selection panels for the NSF fellowship program and hence sophisticated judges, assessed scientific competence in global terms on the basis of a questionnaire requesting diverse kinds of information from the respondents—ranging from the titles and references for publications and a list of the titles of patents granted and pending to the scientist's own estimates of his best accomplishments and a description of the nature of his current job. These overall ratings were found, in turn, to be largely accountable for by reference to a single objective indicator—number of publications.

Whether we consider one or another of the various intelligence and academic achievement assessments as the basis for predicting the raters' evaluations of degree of scientific contribution in the occupational setting, the results are the same. Scientific excellence on the job was essentially unpredictable from earlier information of an academic or intellective nature. If one criticizes this conclusion by pointing out that the selectiveness of the sample results in range restriction for the intellective and academic measures so that some sort of correction for attenuation might be suggested, it can be further pointed out that almost half of the relationships in question—9 of the 24 that were computed—were negative rather than positive in sign. Since corrections for attenuation would increase the size of the negative as well as the positive correlations, the average would still work out to approximately zero—that is, no predictability. In short, there is no doubt that lack of relationship is what the present study demonstrates. As Harmon (1963) puts it, "Most of these coefficients are disappointing. Some of them are negative. Most of them are near zero." (p. 52.)

What does one infer from such results? Harmon's conclusion is to question not the predictors but the criterion. Such a view seems particularly ironic in view of the fact that, while the criterion may be imperfect, it comes considerably closer to what excellence means in real-life functioning than is the case for any of the predictors. The judges, after all, were knowledgeable scientists looking at materials reflective of actual work output, and the judgments were corrected for or protected against various potential sources of rater bias such as systematically rating more stringently or more leniently. In short, great care went into the evaluations of scientific competence: if anything, more care in this study than in many others. Harmon seems concerned with finding that these subjective evaluations hinged so heavily upon the issue of number of publications. On the contrary, however, some degree of prolificness regarding publications is at least a necessary condition for excellence of scientific contribution. Finding that the global judgments were anchored in this kind of objective indicator thus should increase one's confidence in the appropriateness of the subjective assessments. Yet Harmon writes as if the problem has to reside in the criterion because the predictors are above reproach. He seems unable to entertain the possibility that better predictors might be found, but views the situation as one in which we must choose between using predictors of the type described or depending on chance as the way to select students for preferential educational treatment. He sums up the matter in these words: "In spite of these meager findings, I shouldn't say that tossing dice is the way to select Fellows. I think that the trouble is with the criterion measure, in large part" (p. 52). An ideology must be strong indeed if intelligence and academic achievement indicators emerge victorious even though their usefulness in a real-life setting has been found to be nonexistent.

To further underscore the irony, Bloom (1963) has reported work indicating the number of publications produced by academic researchers constituting a good approximation of what he feels can be most appropriately meant by creativity—and Bloom's article appears in the same volume as the Harmon paper. Rather than question productivity as an index of meaningful research attainments, Bloom actually recommended productivity as a particularly useful measuring device in this connection. He came to this conclusion from two lines of evidence. The first concerned a follow-up of 100 University of Chicago candidates who had achieved their Ph.D.'s in diverse fields ranging across the natural and social sciences and the humanities. Considering a period of eight years from date of graduation, Bloom counted the number of publications generated by the members of the sample. His finding was that most of the publishing was done by a small minority of the graduates: less than ten percent accounted for approximately two thirds of the publication output. "One of the possible inferences or conclusions which appear to follow from this pilot study is that, while productivity is clearly not synonymous with creativity, it seems quite likely that unless there is some minimum or threshold of productivity there is little probability or likelihood that the individual is creative" (Bloom, 1963, p. 256). Since publication as such implies the judgment that a standard of quality has been met—a standard that often will be quite high because of the editorial requirements of the publication outlet—Bloom feels that research eminence is pretty well localized within the small proportion of high producers, and therefore that publication output may well constitute an appropriate index of what we can hope to mean by research creativity. Had publication output been evenly spread across the sample, the implication would have been otherwise.

The second line of evidence upon which Bloom drew concerned a sample of chemists and mathematicians who had been chosen as outstandingly creative by panels of their peers—choices for which, incidentally, two independent panels of judges had shown high agreement. The men who had been selected in this manner averaged about 35–40 years of age. To this sample was matched a second sample of chemists and mathematicians who were comparable to the other sample in age, education, and work experience—but had not been judged outstanding contributors to their respective field. The high and low creative samples were compared in terms of performances on a variety of tests of intelligence and of perceptual-cognitive functioning. "Of the 27 tests used in this study, only two yielded significant differences between the two groups, and even for these the hypotheses originally advanced were reversed by the results" (Bloom, 1963, p. 253). Thus, the high creative sample failed to exceed the low creative sample regarding intelligence. On the other hand, the two samples also were compared in terms of number of publications generated over a ten-year period, with the result that the high creative sample was found to average approximately four publications per year while the low creative sample averaged less than one-half a publication per year. Once again, evidence is found supporting the utility of productivity regarding publications as an index of creativity. At the very least, Bloom's work forces us to question the readiness with which Harmon threw out publication output as an accomplishment criterion just because it was not predicted by intelligence or by academic achievement.

The same point emerges again from research reported by MacKinnon (1968). In MacKinnon's work, quality of contribution to their field was judged by knowledgeable peers in the case of samples of research scientists, mathematicians, and architects. Contrasted in each field were comparably mature practitioners of a given profession, differing only in that some were evaluated to have made more distinguished contributions to that profession than did others. MacKinnon administered to these same professionals the Wechsler Adult Intelligence Scale, a conventional means of assessing intelligence. Whether we consider the scientists, the mathematicians, or the architects, no differences regarding intelligence level were found for groups which had been judged to be highly different regarding the importance of what they had contributed to their field. IQ's for all groups averaged about 130. These groups turn out to be quite comparable regarding intelligence variability as well, such variability for all groups ranging from about 120 to 140. MacKinnon notes further that when these people were in high school the grade point averages which they earned there did not show a significant relationship with the degree of their later contribution to their professional field. On the other hand, accomplishments during these earlier years outside of the sphere of academic achievement did, according to MacKinnon, offer a prognosis concerning who would be likely to make substantial contributions to their chosen profession later on.

In a general review of studies such as these, Hoyt (1965; 1966) came to the same overall conclusion that would be suggested by the particular work that we have just considered. On the basis of whatever evidence he could find concerning attempts to study the relationship between grades in college and accomplishment levels in occupations undertaken after formal education, he concluded that little relationship exists. Because of the nature of the available data, his review concentrated upon the occupational categories of scientific research, engineering, business, and medicine. If grades have little predictive power for occupational excellence even in a domain such as scientific research (where one could well expect a heavy dependence upon intellective skills as determinants of successful accomplishment) the same type of outcome would seem all the more likely in the case of occupational endeavors in the arts. All in all, we are left with the startling conclusion that, when viewed in the light of meaningful criteria of life accomplishment, academic grades and the intelligence tests that predict them fare quite poorly within the upper part of the academic skills spectrum.

We must raise the possibility, then, that—in terms of the presumed warrant for their use—tested intelligence and high school grade achievement across the upper part of the distribution receive more attention in the college admissions process than they deserve, although they no doubt provide useful information in the lower part of the distribution. Thus far in regard to accomplishment characteristics of students we have taken note only of high school grades. What of the wide range of talented attainments displayed in varying degrees by secondary school students outside of the academic setting? Not only are these attainments valuable in their own right, but they also may well provide more accurate predictions of who is more likely to display occupational excellence in adulthood than seems to be the case for grades. The student who has served as president of the student body in high school may represent a better bet regarding talent for future political leadership than would the high-grade getter. So also, the student who has published original writings during the high school years may be more likely to demonstrate excellence in writing as an adult than the student whose grade point average is higher. Similar points could be made concerning the student whose artistic talent has been reflected in the winning of awards for pictures exhibited in art competitions, the student whose musical talent has been evidenced by professional performance, and the student whose skill at scientific pursuits has been indicated by his winning recognition in science contests for projects that he carried out in his basement laboratory.

Instances of the kinds just described refer to what the student accomplishes under conditions of maximum autonomy—that is to say, because of spontaneous inclinations on his part more than because of the kinds of extrinsic pressures from school and from parents that could lead to aspiring to higher grades. Such conditions of greater autonomy may be more similar to the life circumstances that typically await a person when he leaves the relatively cloistered and programmed environment of academic studies than is the case for most of what goes on in school. But at the least, we are referring here to what genuinely are accomplishments—to behaviors and products of behavior that, in relatively clear measure, are of intrinsic worth. As we have suggested, this is more than can be said for what usually determines grades.

Collegiate institutions vary in their degree of apparent concern for talented attainments displayed outside the academic program by their applicants, and in their methods of collecting data pertinent to these attainments—if, indeed, they collect such data at all. Some colleges utilize for this purpose the information contained in autobiographical statements made by the applicant. Others rely more heavily on information furnished by school authorities. Holland, Astin, Richards, and their collaborators (see, for example, Holland, 1961; Holland and Astin, 1962; Holland and Nichols, 1964; Holland and Richards, 1965; 1967; Richards, Holland, and Lutz, 1967) have assessed students' talented nonacademic accomplishments by means of check lists on which the student indicates whether he had met a particular criterion of public recognition for a given type of talented activity—such as winning an award in a state or regional debating contest. There is, however, no format commonly accepted among colleges, comparable to that used in the case of intelligence test scores and high school grades, for transmitting information about what a student has accomplished outside of school during his high school years. And if information of this kind *is* obtained, it is used in a way that remains subjective rather than communicable.

Studies concerning such attainments, as conducted with students in the upper part of the academic skills range, lead to the same conclusions as the work on occupational attainments of adults considered before. Thus, talented nonacademic accomplishments were found (Wallach and Wing, 1969) to be fully independent of intelligence test scores and relatively independent of academic achievement in the research by Holland and his coworkers. In the Wallach and Wing research, tested intelligence was substantially related to academic achievement, but not to any of a variety of lines of talented endeavor pursued outside the classroom—including various fields of the arts, science projects, and political leadership. On the other hand, assessments tapping the students' resourcefulness in generating ideas proved to be related to those talent domains that involve production skills—for instance, writing stories or painting pictures—and again quite independent of tested intelligence. In the work by Holland and his colleagues, numerous demonstrations have been provided showing the substantial contrast between the students who excel at academic achievement and the students who excel at various types of talented attainments demonstrated outside the school routine. This work also has found (see Richards, Holland, and Lutz, 1967) that excellence at talented nonacademic accomplishments maintains itself over time, in the sense that students who demonstrate strong attainments of these kinds during high school are more likely to exhibit the same kinds of accomplishments during college.

The foregoing material leads to the conclusion for the upper sector of the academic skills continuum, that talented accomplishments displayed outside of school call attention to a substantially different group of secondary school students than is defined by emphasizing high performance levels within the relatively closed system constituted by intelligence test scores and grade point averages. The intrinsic value of the accomplishments themselves suggests that they merit serious attention in college admissions. They may also offer a better basis for predicting occupational attainments in adult life than is provided by intellective test scores and grades. Yet colleges seem to be quite hard pressed to define either for themselves or for their clientele how they utilize information on talented nonacademic accomplishments.

One general exception to this statement, however, can be cited—demonstrations of athletic prowess during the high school years. A record of talented attainments in athletics often influences the decisions made by college admissions offices. Students of high athletic talent may be accepted even though their intelligence test score and academic achievement credentials are lower than those required of other entering students, and also may be more vigorously recruited in the first place. We have here, then, another exception which seems to prove the rule: colleges appear to place a stronger value on athletics than on art, music, creative writing, or any other kind of talented nonacademic pursuits. Aside from athletics, it is difficult to determine how—or whether—talented accomplishments in the nonacademic world affect the college admissions process. Assessment of these accomplishments may well play a role in a small number of colleges, just as a role also may be played in a few institutions by personality assessments. We suspect, as a matter of fact, that the colleges where nonacademic talented accomplishments, and the colleges where personality considerations play some part in admissions, probably coincide; most likely it is the highly selective colleges that are at issue.

Our survey of student characteristics has left us with the impression that talented nonacademic attainments during the high school years may receive less attention than they deserve, while tested intelligence and academic achievement in high school may receive more attention than they deserve, when it comes to decisions about worthiness for college admission. In terms of their intrinsic merit and their potential prognostic value for adult accomplishments, talented nonacademic attainments during high school seem to be appropriate candidates for serious weight in the admissions process. In terms of their relative lack of meaning in their own right and the surprisingly negative evidence concerning their import at upper levels of academic skills for adult accomplishments, tested intelligence and academic grade level may be exerting a stronger determining influence over admissions than is in fact defensible.

In sum, we believe that talented nonacademic accomplishments are of sufficient intrinsic value to merit heavy weight in the admissions process, provided that the students selected also have shown academic aptitude and grade achievement levels sufficient to qualify them for undertaking college work successfully. We are concerned with those students whose intelligence test scores and grades are in the upper range, and we state that within this range further discriminations as to intelligence and academic achievement are meaningless. Rather than making further distinctions, major attention should be given to talented nonacademic attainments because of their prima facie importance to society. The need for this position arises because we believe—as also does Thresher (1966)—that college admissions presently revolve very tightly around intelligence test scores and high school grades even within this restricted range. Further on we shall provide empirical documentation for this belief. Our critics may argue that there is insufficient evidence for the value of talented nonacademic attainments in predicting career success or cultural contributions in adulthood to warrant their use in student selection at this time. To such critics we reply that the same point is applicable to the predictive utility of intelligence test scores and grades within these upper ranges of academic qualifications. Moreover, contemporary upheavals in college curricula and grading systems suggest the urgency of seeking legitimate indices of talent outside of the conventionally conceived academic domain. The national search for a richer and more diversified definition of the college experience is directly relevant to our search for approaches to talent that take us closer to real-life manifestations.

CHAPTER TWO

College Characteristics
and the Admissions Process

$\mathbf{T}$hus far we have considered just one side of the admissions picture—student characteristics. These characteristics, grouped under the headings of status, personal, and accomplishment characteristics, bear upon the college-going patterns of the nation's high school seniors. Now we turn to the other side of the picture. Each institution of higher education affects the college-going migration by having—whether articulated or not—its own stance, its own attitude, and its own policies toward applicants. A college in effect decides how it will admit or reject those students, with their infinite variety of status, personal, and accomplishment characteristics, who apply for admission. In making its decisions about applicants, therefore, each college sets certain limits upon the migration of students to its doors. Does the student's place of residence play a part? His financial status? His high school record? His intellective test scores? His "personality"? His pattern of accomplishments outside the classroom, however these may be defined? What information about the applicant should be obtained by the admissions office? How should the information be taken into account during the process of deciding yes or no about each candidate? As may be expected from the multiplex of student characteristics and the multiplex of possible policies and practices on the part of institutions, an opportunity is present—in principle—for enormous diversity among colleges as to how decisions will be made.

The way in which emphasis on one student characteristic may interact with concern for another illustrates the complexities that can accumulate as admissions personnel determine their institution's attitude toward applicants. Thus, if a college decides to admit residents of the area on a preferential basis, then it must also take into account how this policy will impinge upon other characteristics of its student body. Will the emphasis on students from the locality have the effect of reducing the degree to which candidates can be chosen on the basis of high intelligence test score qualifications and thereby lower the average test score record of the student body? On the other hand, if a college decides to give heavy emphasis to high test scores, what effect will that policy have on the degree to which students from the nearby region are represented at the college? In dealing with issues such as these, each college hammers out its own way of arriving at decisions. By so doing, it affects in part the total migratory flow of each year's high school graduating class.

Half a century ago, the articulation of college admissions policies was a relatively simple affair. Sufficient space usually was available so that admission could be offered to all students possessing two straightforward status characteristics and qualifying in terms of one accomplishment criterion that in practice was quite easy to meet if the appropriate status characteristics were present. If an applicant could afford to pay the tuition, fees, and residence costs of a college, if he had taken a college preparatory course in high school, and if he had managed to complete his high school curriculum sufficiently well to permit graduation, then the applicant could count on finding a spot in the freshman class of any college he wished to attend. Since few who could pay for an education and were enrolled in a college prep program failed to squeak through, college admission essentially was guaranteed by socioeconomic status. But after World War II, some colleges faced the problem of more applicants than they could accommodate. To try to solve the problem, these institutions sought to define a rational basis—and hence one that they could defend—for making admissions decisions. Without a rational policy to justify the rejection of some applicants, the pain generated by the rejection process would be unmanageable. These institutions also no doubt saw that use of what was thought to be a rational basis for rejecting applicants was a matter of institutional self-interest since it would produce a "higher quality" freshman class. As the number of students seeking college entrance has continued its upward trend since those early postwar years, the pressure felt by colleges to formulate rational-seeming policies for admission has continued to increase as well. For some colleges, the answer has been fairly simple—restriction of enrollment mainly to candidates from the region. For other institutions, however, the situation is much more complex, for they are interested in developing and maintaining a student body that represents a diversity or wide-ranging spectrum of characteristics.

It is impossible to offer a general classification system that will accurately but succinctly describe the admissions policies and practices of all the institutions of higher education in the country. Short of constructing the composite photograph that would result from combining all the various admissions practices, coupled with all the various policy statements—an enterprise that in any case would be more confusing than clarifying—our task is to abstract some pivotal distinctions among the colleges as to how they cope with admissions. We know that there are differences in this regard. What we want to do is point out some broad contrasts to show what institutions are like. Our aim is to survey the terrain in such a manner that we will know where to focus later on.

Admissions policies followed by colleges are not, whatever may be the pressures to formulate them, by and large fully rational and explicitly delineated. If they were, the admissions process would be carried out in a relatively straightforward manner, and our task of classification would be easier. Possession of a rational policy would mean that the goals of that policy could be articulated for implementation in practice by a given companion strategy. Once the strategy had been put into effect, the characteristics of the group of students gaining admission could be examined in order to check if the policy goals had been achieved. For instance, suppose a college decided to eliminate all candidates who had ranked within the bottom three-fourths of their high school class. It would be easy enough to determine whether that policy had been put into practice simply by examining the high school records of those admitted. Most colleges, however, for a variety of reasons that we shall discuss later, are loathe to force a completely rational policy upon their admissions practices and, as a result, their approaches are bound to be rough and approximate. So must be our descriptive classification of the institutions.

An initial degree of clarity concerning the kinds of admissions policies formulated and practices carried out on the college scene will result, we feel, from a consideration of three general approaches, each of which is typical of a different group of collegiate institutions. Since the typology to be set forth has been designed to describe different policies and practices, the number of colleges represented in each of the three groups is allowed to fall where it may, and in fact turns out to vary across the groups. As was the case in our consideration of student characteristics in Chapter 1, we shall first outline and define our classification of college characteristics, and then proceed to a more detailed discussion of each type of institution.

A first group of colleges can be discerned that virtually has its doors open to everybody. We can describe these institutions as *minimally selective*. To call their admissions policy an open one is not to assert a complete absence of admissions criteria, but to say that the requirements for entrance are at once specific and easy to meet. Thus, for example, institutions of this type will declare that they will accept all students with a high school diploma who reside within the state—up to the limits of available space. If they run out of space, they seek to expand their facilities rather than deny admission to a candidate who meets their acceptance requirements. Most of the minimally selective institutions are public, and, in their case, stated policies and actual practices are consistent. The private institutions in this group, however, often seek to maintain an image of more than minimal selectivity while at the same time actively recruiting all minimally qualified prospects. In contrast to these minimally selective colleges, two other groups of colleges can be delineated that vary in terms of the stringency of their selectivity; refer to them as *moderately selective* and *highly selective* institutions.

Moderately selective institutions are those which accept a majority of the students who apply to them. It is our impression that those candidates who are rejected tend to be eliminated chiefly on the basis of low intelligence test scores and low secondary school grade records. The majority of the moderately selective institutions are private and tend to put forth descriptions of admissions policies which emphasize a multiplicity of characteristics as governing a student's acceptability. Policy descriptions thus espouse diversity, tending for the most part to suggest that selection depends upon a variety of desired qualifications, including various status, personal, and accomplishment attributes, with the goal of establishing a variegated student body. To the extent that official policy espouses diversity while actual admissions practices stress the personal characteristic of intelligence test scores and the accomplishment characteristic of high school grades as the only real considerations, much less is required of prospective enrollees than the catalogues imply.

By highly selective institutions, finally, we refer to those which accept only a minority of applicants. These are the colleges of national prestige, and they have, in the last 20 years, become heavily oversubscribed. Once again, the majority of the colleges in this category are private and tend to suggest in their descriptions of admissions policies that decisions to admit or reject candidates turn on a considerable variety of student characteristics. While this seems to be true in the case of some, our impression is that, once again, most of the institutions in this category emphasize in their selection practices the applicants' intelligence test scores and academic achievement levels in high school. That is to say, for only a small minority of the colleges in this category do we believe it is the case, for instance, that a student who is valedictorian of his high school class and has very high tested intelligence may be rejected in favor of a candidate who has more modest intellective and academic achievement qualifications but who has evidenced unusual accomplishments in some line of pursuit that is defined as extracurricular because it does not contribute to a grade point average. To the degree that admissions policy statements enumerate a heterogeneous range of status, personal, and accomplishment characteristics as what these colleges are seeking in their students, while actual selection hinges heavily upon intelligence test scores and high school grades, then once more a gap exists between stated policies and the practices that are carried out.

Minimally Selective Institutions

Having defined American colleges as falling roughly into three groups—minimally selective, moderately selective, and highly selective—we would like to say a bit more about each type. We return first to those institutions that we described as minimally selective. Since, by definition, these open-door institutions are available to virtually all applicants, their admissions policies and practices tend to encourage the flow of high school graduates to college. A majority of these institutions are publicly supported, but some of them are private colleges that serve local areas and restricted clienteles. Typically, they have recently emerged on the higher education scene—their numbers having expanded at a rapid pace during the last five to ten years. In this category are junior colleges, community colleges, and some little-known private and parochial colleges. Also, in the case of the less populous states, are some institutions that carry a university designation. The community and junior colleges, however, constitute the majority of the present category's membership. The growth spurt in the number of minimally selective institutions founded in recent years represents a direct response to the growing sector of the population which demands that college-going opportunities be made available. Most of the students who attend these colleges live within commuting distance. The costs incurred by attendance are usually minimal. With the typical student at such a college continuing to reside at home, the level of expenditure required of the family will be only slightly higher than that they paid to send their child to public high school.

The educational resources provided by the minimally selective institutions tend to be ranked at the low end of the prestige hierarchy, whether viewed in terms of facilities-oriented yardsticks such as the number of books in the library or in terms of faculty-oriented measures such as the number of faculty members with Ph.D. degrees. The student populations served by these colleges, while tending to be nearer average and therefore lower on intelligence and high school rank measures than students attending more selective institutions, nevertheless represent a wide range of academic proficiency. Most of these students attended public secondary schools, come from families of middle or lower-middle socio-economic status, and are the first generation in their families to attend college. The career goals of students at these colleges tend to be concretely vocational in nature, and so also are the kinds of curricula that such colleges offer.

When it comes to the stated admissions policies at the unselective colleges, explicit emphasis is given to the open-door nature of the institution. A student thus has virtually no problem at all in estimating his likelihood of gaining admission. He knows that his acceptance is assured if, for instance, he lives in a particular geographic region and is a high-school graduate whose course of study has included a minimum college preparatory program. While they are not used for admissions purposes, tests of intellective aptitude and the level of academic achievement in high school may, on the other hand, be used for placement purposes after enrollment. How many colleges fall within this minimally selective category? A large proportion—probably 900 or 1000—of the more than 2000 institutions of higher education in the nation.

Moderately Selective Institutions

Next we turn to those institutions which accept a majority of their applicants—the moderately selective colleges. Requirements for admission to these colleges usually include not just any kind of secondary school diploma, but one which reflects rather carefully specified units of college preparatory coursework—as compared with relatively little definition concerning particular high school coursework required for admission to the minimally selective colleges. The level of secondary school grades attained by the student, moreover, is usually taken into account, and scores on tests of intellective aptitude are required along with the high school record. In our estimation, the customary aim of the admissions officers at these colleges is to reject those candidates who seem to lack sufficient academic preparation or who have demonstrated on intelligence tests what seems like an insufficient level of academic aptitude. These colleges typically eliminate, on the foregoing grounds, an average of about 25 percent of their applicants—with the bulk of those rejected ranging from 10 percent to 40 percent. The implicit decision rule seems to be "Accept the candidate, unless rejection is required by virtue of low academic aptitude or low academic performance."

How are the moderately selective institutions distributed across the public and private sectors of the higher education system? Both sectors are represented, with the private institutions in the majority. The private colleges in this category are likely to be small liberal arts colleges, colleges with a religious affiliation, or metropolitan universities serving a regional clientele. They differ from their sister institutions in the minimally selective category by being already better known and by describing themselves as more selective and more interested in diversity in the student body. The public institutions that fit this classification usually have been in existence for 40 years or more and have recently undergone changes in response to rising demands for higher education. The changes include increasing their enrollment markedly and changing their name from, for example, "state college for teachers" to "state university." Occasionally included among these public institutions may be the major university in a state—but not one that has been traditionally accorded a position of national prominence.

As to yardsticks such as the number of Ph.D.'s on the faculty or the size of the library, these institutions rank higher than the minimally selective colleges. The moderately selective colleges are not, however, the prominent or prestigious ones on the national scene. Costs of attending these colleges are greater than those for the minimally selective colleges. In the case of the moderately selective colleges that are privately supported—which, as we noted, constitute the majority of the category—student tuition payments are apt to provide a major financial bulwark. Filling the freshman class at these private institutions is therefore of crucial importance to the college's economic survival, and selection must be sacrificed to the budget. The frequent result of this financial imperative is the presence of vigorous recruiting programs aimed at soliciting students who will meet admissions requirements. While financial aid from the federal government or the college may help offset the expenses of attending moderately selective private institutions in the case of some students, the amounts charged for tuition, fees, and living expenses (where the latter are involved) constitute for many a distinct barrier. Whether the institution is private or public, however, student bodies in moderately selective institutions tend to come from middle-class and upper-middle-class backgrounds. The parents, by implication, are likely to have a record of at least some college attendance. Most of the students will have attended public secondary schools. The students are predominantly from the region where the college is located, or one nearby, but typically they live on the campus rather than commuting from home.

How do the moderately selective colleges state their admissions policies? On the whole, it is our impression that a general distinction exists regarding the kinds of explicit statements offered by the private moderately selective institutions—which, as mentioned before, constitute the majority of the category—and the minority that are public. The public institutions tend to make policy statements that seem to reflect with reasonable accuracy the nature of their practices: catalogues will indicate that attainment of particular intellective test scores and of particular levels of high school academic performance are required or preferred, and that these comprise the basic hurdles which the student has to surmount. The private colleges, on the other hand, often suggest in their official pronouncements that they are looking for students who possess a variety of status, personal, and accomplishment characteristics in addition to intellective test score and academic achievement credentials. Thus, for example, a typical published catalogue might assert: "We are seeking students who represent a diversity of backgrounds and inter-ests—students who will care about more than grades and will make a creative contribution to campus life." The point is made that careful consideration will be given to a complex and multifaceted set of student characteristics before deciding to admit or to reject. We suspect that these claims diverge drastically from the actual admissions practices at these institutions, in that adequate grades and intelligence test scores are sufficient to win acceptance—provided that the candidate's family can foot the bill.

Our considered estimate is that there are some 850 to 950 colleges and universities in this moderately selective category—nearly half of the institutions of higher education in the country. The curricula that they offer are usually oriented around four-year degree programs in the liberal arts, but there is also a goodly amount of work available in such profes-sional areas as engineering, education, and business administration.

Highly Selective Institutions

Consider finally those institutions that fall within the highly selective category—those that reject more than 50 percent of their appli-cants. From our starting pool of over 2000 institutions, we now are down to perhaps 150 to 180 as the number that can claim membership in this third rubric. With more applicants rejected than accepted, the typical rejection rate for colleges and universities in this category is by our esti-mate something on the order of 60 percent, and the rejection rate for some runs more than 80 percent. Like the moderately selective institu-tions, the majority of those in the highly selective category are privately supported. Together, these private and public institutions comprise the nationally prominent sources of higher education in the country. The private ones hold regional positions of high prestige together with a high national ranking, while the minority that are public tend to be the queen institutions of their state systems. In terms of curricula, these schools range across the liberal arts, the sciences, and preprofessional training in such fields as law and medicine. Their student bodies come mainly from the upper-middle class, although a growing minority derives from more humble origins. Private school backgrounds, while not in the majority, may represent significant proportions on many of these campuses—even rising as high as half on a few. For the most part the students are second generation college-goers. They come from all over the nation to attend these colleges, which are almost entirely residential in character. Such commuting as does occur is likely to be between the campus and a town apartment rented in preference to a dormitory room.

With regard to cost, the highly selective institutions vary widely between those in the private and those in the public sectors, and for the latter there is a further distinction between costs for in-state and for out-of-state students. To students who reside within the state, the public institutions are of moderate cost; to out-of-state students they are expensive. The private colleges and universities, in turn, are almost always high in cost. Considerable financial aid is made available at the highly selective institutions, with the result that anywhere from 30 percent to 50 percent of the student body receive some form of such aid, whether as gifts, loans, or employment. Indeed, costs are such that even students from middle-class backgrounds often find themselves in need of financial assistance—although they could, of course, have attended a minimally selective college without financial strain.

In delineating their admissions policies, a broad distinction once again emerges between the statements made by the private and by the public institutions—keeping in mind further that for the highly selective as for the moderately selective schools, the private institutions outnumber the public ones. On the whole, explicit policy descriptions for the highly selective private institutions seem to parallel those for the moderately selective private institutions, and a similar parallelism prevails for the highly and moderately selective public institutions.

Thus, the private institutions describe themselves as vitally interested in a wide variety of student characteristics over and beyond intelligence test scores and high school grades. The desirability of various extracurricular attainments, for example, will be emphasized in describing what is taken into account when admissions decisions are made. By contrast, the public institutions set forth their admissions policy (for in-state students) as resting frankly on measures of academic aptitude and academic achievement. They may indicate, for example, that they will accept to the limit of space available all students residing in the state who rank within the top ten percent of their high school class. No doubt the public institutions formulate their admissions policy in terms of strictly academic yardsticks because criteria of that kind are most readily defensible to state legislatures. Consideration of other credentials or other potential kinds of talents is much harder to explain at the state capital, because admitting students on the basis of such factors may give the appearance of yielding to some pressure group—whether the pressure might arise from art buffs, newspaper editors, or the state music teachers' association. When it comes to out-of-state applicants, on the other hand— and such applicants will be held to a minority quota—statements about what is looked for tend to resemble the kind of broad-gauged search for diverse characteristics that we have described as typical of the highly selective private institutions.

Standard tests of academic aptitude as well as records of secondary school grades almost always are required for admissions consideration at any of the highly selective institutions, whether private or public. In addition, especially the private colleges and universities in this category pursue various further means of candidate assessment in their desire to implement the policy goal of considering a diversity of status, personal, and accomplishment characteristics in the admissions process. For example, alumni often are organized into elaborate networks to assist the admissions staff by interviewing candidates and attempting to rate them in various ways, and extensive information about a wide range of characteristics is requested from the applicants. In general, the applicants to institutions in the highly selective category tend to be self-selected to a certain degree regarding high school grades and intelligence-test scores, since candidates believe that they stand no chance at all of admission unless they are above some kind of threshold in these regards. Consequently, viewed in national perspective, the applicant pool itself from which the highly selective institutions make their choices already can be characterized as the cream of the academic-aptitude and academic-achievement crop. From this point of view, it would be rational indeed to pursue policies aimed at gathering in students of diverse and heterogeneous characteristics, as is the stated claim of the highly selective private institutions. For we are dealing with applicants who are located in above-average ranges on indicators of intellective skill and academic achievement in the first place.

We do know, of course, that in the case of certain small groups of students who do not meet the usual academic standards, policy at highly selective institutions still allows for admission. Such exceptions most notably may be made in the case of applicants who have skills to display on Saturday afternoons before large crowds. Some exceptions also may be made for students who come from culturally different or disadvantaged backgrounds. Apart from special recruitment efforts directed toward such groups, however, superior intelligence-test and grade-level credentials are needed at the outset for admissions consideration at these schools, and students who lack these credentials in question usually do not bother to apply.

With something on the order of 150 to 180 institutions belonging to the highly selective category, these colleges and universities constitute only a small percentage of the more than 2000 institutions of higher education in the country. Yet the influence of the admissions policies and practices of this small minority is very great on the rest of the higher education scene because of the strong prestige they enjoy in the public view. Their popularity has led them, in the face of increasing demand over the years, to a stiffening of admission standards with respect to academic aptitude and academic achievement. The consequence has been an overflow of applicants downward to the moderately selective and minimally selective institutions, whose growth has thereby been fostered. Whereas in former days those colleges and universities that would presently be named as members of the highly selective category provided the bulk of the available collegiate opportunities to the nation's high school graduates, they now offer a relatively small proportion of the total number of college slots. This proportion comprises however the educational opportunities that are most strenuously contested. Having covered the explicit policies of these elite institutions with respect to admissions, can we determine how these policies are fulfilled in their practices?

Of the institutions qualifying for elite status, we have noted that the majority are privately supported, and that their admissions policy suggests that they are interested in a diversity of student attributes when deciding whom to admit. In other words, that they are interested not only in the highest intelligence scorers and those with the most superlative records of academic achievement, but also in the applicants who have demonstrated unusual attainments outside the conventional school environment—in such areas as political leadership, art, music, creative writing, dramatics, or self-developed scientific investigations. Indeed, it is just this kind of explicit emphasis on a search for diversity that provides the model for private institutions in the moderately selective category to follow in framing their own policy statements. And, as we have said, most of the colleges and universities in the moderately selective as well as in the highly selective categories are private rather than public. And we have suggested that such emphases on searching out diversity when making their selections are inconsistent with the actual practices at private institutions in the moderately selective category, admission depending rather on little more than adequate secondary school grades and a high enough score on a test of scholastic aptitude. Since these schools by definition accept more applicants than they reject (and in fact need all the students they can accommodate in order to survive financially) one surmises that, while their catalogues may talk diversity because it is fashionable to do so, the main qualifications needed to gain admission are the test scores and the grades.

Regarding actual practices at the highly selective private institutions, in turn, our estimate is that only a handful—perhaps 30 or so—practice to a serious degree the diversity which they seem to preach. This would leave the majority claiming that they emphasize diverse criteria in selecting students but in fact emphasizing test scores and grades despite the already high level of these credentials—for example, SAT scores falling within the top half of the national distribution for high school seniors who go on to college—possessed by most of the members of their applicant pool. The basis for this estimate is admittedly intuitive since data on the subject are almost nonexistent. It is precisely because of this state of affairs that we conducted the research described later in this book concerning ways of defining the talents of a given year's applicants to a typical private institution in the highly selective category.

In the present chapter we have provided an overview of the institutional side of the admissions filter. Having described in Chapter 1 the characteristics of the students who seek admission to the nation's colleges and universities, we turned in the chapter at hand to a description of what the institutions are like that offer higher educational opportunities. From the latter overview we have glimpsed the possibility that considerable discrepancies exist between explicitly formulated admissions policies and actual admissions practices. We have also seen, however, that little by way of hard data regarding the interplay between applicant characteristics and admissions decisions were around to guide us, with the result that our account had to be speculative and impressionistic. In the next chapter we attempt to remedy this lack by examining information that casts light on how admissions decisions actually are made. Then, after a chapter discussing why admissions practices at the highly selective institutions are of particular importance, we turn to a second and much more detailed empirical investigation. That investigation will concern extensive assessment of a considerable range of applicant characteristics as these relate to the admissions process at a typical highly selective institution.

CHAPTER THREE

Are Admissions Decisions Predictable?
A First Systematic Look

We can now begin to explore how particular types of colleges react to particular characteristics of students when deciding whom to accept and whom to reject. Objective evidence on this question—in contrast to opinion or folklore—has been scant indeed. Goslin (1967), for example, has noted that ". . . data on the use of test scores, as opposed to the extent of test giving, are extremely difficult to come by." (p. 15.) Given this paucity of explicit information about how colleges make their admissions decisions, the customary way of answering the question has been to find out what the admissions office of a college tells you it does. Accurate appraisal on a subjective basis of a matter as complicated and as affect-laden as that of arriving at admissions decisions, however, clearly is fraught with difficulties. We feel that we are on very safe ground, then, when we suggest—as we did in the preceding chapter—that what actually happens often may deviate considerably from what the interested parties think or believe is going on.

In the absence of firm documentation, though, such a suggestion means little. The present chapter therefore takes a first systematic look at what actually happens by considering the degree to which admissions decisions can be predicted on the basis of very elementary information about candidate characteristics. We will analyze material concerning (1) a representative national sample of collegiate institutions ranging across the moderately and highly selective categories; (2) a representative national sample of institutions confined to the highly selective category; (3) a highly selective college that has recently shifted toward greater diversity; and (4) a typical college in the highly selective category for which we have more detailed information than in the case of the national sample of highly selective institutions. The orientation of our inquiry in this chapter is one of accounting for the status quo—describing roughly what goes on. In the case of the college that has shifted toward greater diversity, however, we will start moving toward the issue of what alternative admissions practices *might* go on; in other words, what the possibilities are for change regarding how admissions decisions are reached.

Form of the Relationship between SAT-V Score
and Percentage of Applicants Accepted

In order to obtain for representative national samples of institutions information that would aid us in our quest, we had recourse to source materials reported by colleges to the College Entrance Examination Board and collated by the Board in their *Manual of Freshman Class Profiles, 1965–1967* (College Entrance Examination Board, 1965). The *Manual* includes reports from 419 colleges on the classes they accepted in the spring of 1964 for admission the following fall. Two hundred and twenty-four colleges presented data showing the number of applications

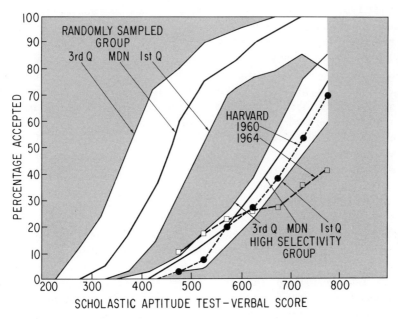

Percentage of applicants accepted as a function of SAT-V score in the randomly sampled group of colleges, the high-selectivity group of colleges, Harvard for 1960, and Harvard for 1964.

they received and the number of candidates they accepted. The data were arranged according to 50-point score intervals on the verbal section of the Scholastic Aptitude Test (SAT-V). This verbal aptitude measure constitutes, of course, a frequently encountered index of general intelligence. We had in hand therefore materials enabling us to study for an array of institutions the bearing of a particular personal characteristic— namely, the intelligence of the candidates as estimated from SAT-V scores —on the admissions decision-making practiced at these institutions.

We drew two samples from these 224 colleges. The first was a 20 percent random sample, yielding 45 colleges. Since colleges of the mini- mally selective type are unlikely to be members of the College Entrance Examination Board (which means they will not be listed in the *Manual*) and since the levels of selectivity found among the 224 colleges span a wide range, this random sample represents institutions in the moderately and the highly selective categories. For each of the 45 colleges in the ran- dom sample, we considered the total applicant pool as a unit—disregard- ing the sex of the applicants and whether they had public or private high school backgrounds. For any given institution we computed the per- centage of the applicant group accepted in each 50-point score interval for the SAT-V. The median values of these percentages of candidates accepted for each SAT-V score interval and the interquartile ranges are graphed in the accompanying figure. The number of institutions included varies somewhat from one SAT-V score interval to another because some colleges in the sample received no applications from candidates scoring within certain intervals. In a few cases, colleges lumped all candidates scoring below a particular level into one category. Such cases were han- dled by computing the percentage of acceptances for the group in ques- tion and placing that percentage in the highest applicable score interval. For example, if an institution reported all applicants who earned SAT-V scores below 400 as one group, the percentage of acceptances from that group was assigned to the 350–399 score interval and the institution was not counted for score intervals below the 350 level.

In contrast to the first sample, whose members ranged from moderate to high levels of selectivity, the second sample drawn was a set of 13 col- leges confined to the highly selective category. Using the work of Astin (1965) as a basis for arriving at an independent definition of high selec- tivity, we identified from among the more than 1000 institutions upon which Astin reported the 26 that comprised the top $2\frac{1}{2}$ percent of his group with regard to admissions selectivity. Of the 26 schools in question, 13 were found among the 224 colleges presenting the aforementioned kind of raw materials on SAT-V scores as collected in the *Manual* (College Entrance Examination Board, 1965). The median figure for percentage of candidates accepted among the colleges in this high-selectivity sample turned out to be 37 percent—just a bit more selective than the figure of 40 percent that we gave as an approximate average for the category of highly selective institutions defined in Chapter 2, but certainly acceptable as a rough approximation to a representative national sample of institu- tions in the high-selectivity category. By contrast, the random sample of 45 institutions was found to yield a percentage figure of 65 percent for the proportion of applicants accepted at the median institution. This indi- cated considerably less selectivity for a sample assumed to range across the moderately and highly selective categories. At the same time it showed greater selectivity than the figure of 75 percent mentioned in Chapter 2 as an approximate average for institutions comprising the moderate-selectivity category alone. In order to maximize the difference between the two kinds of samples, it seemed desirable for the high-selectivity sample to stand on the more selective side of the central tendency value of 40 percent offered on an a priori basis in the preceding chapter's delineation of the high-selectivity category. The figure contains for the high-selectivity sample of 13 schools the same information described for the random sample of 45.

What is indicated by the data displayed in the figure? Consider first the sample of institutions that range from moderate to high selectivity—the random sample. We can note immediately the wide variability among the institutions in this sample regarding the percentages of applicants accepted at any given SAT-V score interval. At the 400–449 score interval, for example, almost 60 percentage points in terms of proportions of applicants accepted separate the first and third quartiles. Institutions at and above the third quartile are the 25 percent that are least selective in the sample, while institutions at and below the first quartile are the 25 percent that are most highly selective. Thus a candidate's migration from high school to college depends not only on his SAT-V score level, but also on the institution to which he applies. If his SAT-V score is within the 400–449 interval and he applies to a college that falls at or above the third quartile, the odds for favorable action on his application are 7 to 3 or better; while if, with the same SAT-V score, he applies to a college that is located at or below the first quartile, then the odds are more than 8 to 2 that he will be rejected.

Despite the kind of selection variability just described, however, the figure also displays for the random sample of colleges a highly systematic positive relationship between the magnitude of SAT-V scores and the proportion of the applicant population accepted for admission. For example, although institutions that fall at the third quartile are not overly selective concerning the SAT-V score level demanded, it still is the case, for an institution of this type, that the higher the candidate's SAT-V score, the more likely he will be accepted. The same sort of positive relationship is found for institutions at the median in selectivity as well as for colleges located at the first quartile. Regardless of the different levels of selectivity in the institutions in this random sample, they turn out to show something in common: a consistent positive relationship between an estimate of the applicant's intelligence level and his chances of gaining admission. That the varied institutions across the selectivity spectrum all share this functional relationship makes the point that the relatively selective as well as the relatively unselective colleges place emphasis upon SAT-V scores in deciding which applicants to accept.

Let us turn now to the independently defined sample of high-selectivity institutions that we developed on the basis of Astin's research. Does the information graphed in the figure for this second sample offer further confirmation for the generalization made above? The answer is yes. There is, first of all, a rather marked decline in selection variability below SAT-V scores of 650 among the colleges in this high-selectivity sample as compared to the colleges in the random sample. This fact is, of course, quite expectable from the much greater homogeneity of the former sample. The lower variability for the highly selective sample—that is, the reduced interquartile range—indicates a rather consistent pattern of rejecting candidates who score below something on the order of 600 for the SAT-V. Yet—and this is the crucial point—the shapes of the curves plotted in relating SAT-V score level to proportion of applicants accepted for the high-selectivity sample seem to come from the same family as the curve shapes that emerge for the random sample. This is so, even though the curves for the two samples reflect the sharp distinction that exists between them in acceptance rates. The chances for acceptance systematically increase for both samples as the SAT-V score increases. For instance, likelihood of acceptance increases more than fourfold between SAT-V score levels of 350–399 and 550–599 in the random sample, while increases of this same magnitude are found between score levels of 500–549 and 700–749 in the high-selectivity sample. In effect, the functions slide over about 150 points along the SAT-V continuum, but remain comparable in shape.

To sum up what we have learned thus far: Regardless of how selective a college may be, a consistent positive relationship holds between SAT-V score and likelihood of acceptance. The difference between institutions with lower and higher levels of selectivity seems to reside not as much in the degree to which they depend upon SAT-V scores in making their admissions decisions—although there are some differences in this regard and we will consider them later in the chapter—as in the level of SAT-V scores required. No matter how stringent the selectivity, in other words, the fact is that higher SAT-V scores serve to improve a candidate's prospects for acceptance.

Consider, by contrast, what we should find if a college actually is utilizing decisional criteria that make for greater diversity in their admissions approach—criteria that provide information about valued student characteristics beyond what turns out simply to co-vary with intelligence level. We should find that the positive relationship between SAT-V score level and proportion of candidates accepted evens off above some threshold zone of SAT-V performance. This flattening out of the function relating SAT-V scores and probability of acceptance should occur because above whatever general degree of intelligence is believed to represent a sufficient indication of competence in that direction, the weight given to other considerations should increase markedly. To that extent the acceptance or rejection of the candidate should not become more predictable from knowing the degree of further increment of his SAT-V score above the hypothetical threshold value. But we have found that probability of acceptance keeps increasing. In the high-selectivity sample of institutions, for example, candidates in the 700–749 range of SAT-V scores are fully three times more likely to be accepted than candidates scoring in the 550–599 range. Yet scores in the 550–599 range already are relatively high—around the 80th percentile for those high school seniors who later enter college.

Can the sort of leveling off just considered actually be found in some particular instance? From the data presented thus far we would expect it to be a rare phenomenon, since we have been hard put to find evidence for it in the national samples of institutions that we have surveyed. Our discussion in Chapter 2 did suggest, however, that the frequently encountered claims by high-selectivity institutions of practicing diversity in admissions possess a substantial basis in fact for a minority of the colleges in that category. One such case seems to be Harvard, where a concerted effort has been made over the last few years to relax the emphasis on high intelligence-test scores and increase the emphasis on student characteristics other than those that are intelligence-related as bases for making admissions decisions.

Whitla (1968) has recently presented data showing, for a period of years, the same kind of information in the case of Harvard as we have been describing in the case of national samples of institutions—namely, the percentage of candidates accepted as a function of various SAT-V score intervals. On the basis of these Harvard data we have constructed the graphs for Harvard presented in the figure, which are to be interpreted in the same manner as the graphs already described. Shown is a comparison between the functional relationships linking SAT-V score level and likelihood of acceptance for two applicant populations to Harvard separated in time by four years: applicants for admission for the fall of 1960 and applicants for admission for the fall of 1964. Whitla argues that during this period a change took place in Harvard's use of admissions criteria so as to give greater weight to other kinds of student attributes than intelligence and its correlates. To the extent that a change of this kind actually did take place, Harvard would constitute an illustration of a highly selective institution that had moved in the direction of increased diversity in its approach to admissions, and this move should be reflected in a comparison of the 1960 and 1964 functions presented in the figure. The prediction would be that the Harvard 1960 function should resemble the functions shown for highly selective colleges in the figure, while the

Harvard 1964 function should show the kind of leveling off that we have already described. Remember that the national data summarized in the figure pertain to classes admitted for the fall of 1964, so we are testing whether Harvard at that recent point in time was deviating from the contemporary national pattern as well as from its own earlier pattern, which in turn we expect to approximate the described national pattern.

The prediction just offered is supported by the graphs of the two Harvard classes. Note first the function for the class that Harvard admitted for the fall of 1960. We find once again the same systematic rise in proportion of candidates accepted as a function of increasing levels of SAT-V scores that we are familiar with from considering the national sample of high selectivity colleges shown in the figure. In fact, all points for the Harvard 1960 function, except those for SAT-V scores under 500, fall within the interquartile ranges presented for the highly selective colleges. Clearly, therefore, the admissions practices reflected in the Harvard 1960 function closely approximate those followed by the national sample of highly selective institutions in 1964. When, however, we examine the Harvard 1964 function, the curve gives evidence of a rather dramatic change in the relationship between SAT-V scores and favorable admissions action. The proportion of candidates accepted in SAT-V score intervals of 650 and up has declined markedly, and this decline has been accompanied by a comparable increase in acceptances from the score intervals below 600. In 1960, by way of example, an applicant scoring in the 750–800 interval on the SAT-V had a chance of acceptance that was more than three times greater than that for an applicant scoring in the 550–599 interval. Four years later, on the other hand, a score in the 750–800 interval did not even double the likelihood of acceptance compared to the chances for someone scoring in the 550–599 interval. Thus, unlike the earlier Harvard data and unlike also the situation prevailing in 1964 for the national sample of highly selective institutions, Harvard in 1964 was downplaying the importance of SAT-V score levels in favor of placing greater weight upon other considerations.

Having considered the functional relationship between SAT-V level and the probability of acceptance, we find that the relationship in question is strongly positive throughout the range of measurement. The shift over time that has been demonstrated for Harvard shows how a policy change toward lessened emphasis on SAT-V scores becomes reflected in a changed form of relationship: namely, a flattening of the slope. By illustrating the way in which this kind of graph can change its shape, the Harvard shift underscores the meaning of what is shown in the figure for the national samples of institutions. While analyzing the form of the relationship between SAT-V score level and candidate acceptability has been illuminating, however, there is another way of describing the college admissions decision-making process that can make even more clear the extent to which it turns upon very limited kinds of information about applicant characteristics. We can consider the proportion of decisions that are correctly predicted by applying a particular specified rule for deciding upon the acceptability of candidates. To the extent that applying a simple rule generates a high proportion of correct predictions concerning actual admissions actions, we will have demonstrated that such actions can to that degree be accounted for in terms of whatever the rule deals with.

Predicting Admissions Actions by Applying a Hypothetical Decision Rule

Let us be more concrete about what we have in mind. Suppose we suspect that most of what actually goes on in making admissions decisions can be understood simply by taking account of a single item of information about the applicant—his SAT-V score. If we are right about this, then a hypothetical decision strategy, set up in a manner to rely upon SAT-V scores in deciding whom to accept and whom to reject should agree with the empirical decisions made by the admissions committees of the various colleges. Another way of saying this is that the hypothetical decision strategy should substantially reduce the error that would otherwise be made in predicting what action will be taken on a student's application for admission.

We began at the point just described, formulating hypothetical policies simply on the basis of SAT-V score and seeing how well our predictions would stack up against the empirical pattern of acceptances and rejections. Actually, a second item of information had to enter into our formula—information about the college rather than about the candidate. We had to know the proportion of applicants accepted for admission by each college under consideration. This knowledge was imperative if our hypothetical strategy was to constitute a legitimate model for predicting admissions decisions. In an institution that rejects 90 percent of its applicants, for example, we could be correct 90 times in 100 simply by predicting rejection of all candidates. The college would be left, however, with no freshman class at all—clearly an unrealistic and inadmissible outcome. A legitimate hypothetical strategy, therefore, obviously must develop its decisions on the basis of accepting and rejecting the respective numbers of students that are appropriate in terms of the educational goals and space requirements of the given college. For each college under consideration we set the proportion of candidates accepted by our hypothetical decision strategy to be the same as that accepted by the college. After setting this quota, we applied the following strategy:

Rank all candidates on the basis of their SAT-V scores, and accept them in order of decreasing rank until the acceptance quota for that college is filled. This rule quite directly stipulates that only a candidate's SAT-V score will be taken into account in deciding whether to admit or reject him. We may call it the "SAT-V" strategy.

To illustrate, if a college accepted 30 percent of its applicants, we listed the applicants on the basis of their SAT-V scores. We grouped them in 50-point intervals, because that is the form in which these data were available, and predicted acceptance of those students whose SAT-V scores fell within the top 30 percent and rejection of the rest. Where the number of candidates needed to meet the rule's acceptance quota fell within an SAT-V score interval, we took the number of candidates required by the quota and assumed that the proportions accepted and rejected by the college for the interval as a whole also applied to this subset.

We applied this hypothetical SAT-V strategy to the various colleges considered thus far: the national sample of 45 randomly chosen institutions, the national sample of 13 colleges in the highly selective category, and Harvard, examining the frequencies accepted and rejected in actuality above and below the strategy's cut-off point. We then went on to apply this and related hypothetical strategies to an institution for which we had more extensive data on an individual candidate basis and which we had reason to believe was typical of those in the highly selective category—namely, Duke. In all of these cases we examined the admissions decisions actually made by the colleges in order to determine the extent of agreement between the hypothetical actions based upon a given strategy and the empirical actions that were actually taken. Note the four possible outcomes that can result from applying a hypothetical admissions strategy to a set of actual admissions decisions—two of agreement between hypothetical rule and actual practice, and two of disagreement: (1) the hypothetical strategy accepts the candidate and so does the admissions committee of the college; (2) the hypothetical strategy rejects the candidate and so does the college; (3) the hypothetical strategy accepts the candidate but the college rejects him; and (4) the hypothetical strategy rejects the candidate but the college accepts him.

Let us return first to the data for the random sample, the high-selectivity sample, and Harvard. For each college in both of the national samples, and for Harvard on each of the two occasions considered earlier, we computed the proportion of the applicants for whom decisions made by our hypothetical SAT-V strategy and by the college were in agreement—either because there was acceptance both by the SAT-V strategy and by the college, or because there was rejection both by the SAT-V strategy and by the college. The values for these computations of percent decisions in agreement are given for the median, first quartile, and third quartile institutions in each of the two national samples, as well as for Harvard, in Table 3.1. We also computed for these same institutions the proportion of *acceptances* for which the hypothetical strategy agreed with the class actually selected—that is, the percent acceptances in agreement. Those entries also appear in Table 3.1. In addition, the table reports the results for a statistical index which expresses the degree to which the rate of error expected by chance is reduced by applying the hypothetical strategy in question—an error-reduction index. When a particular quota of individuals is drawn twice from the same total population—with the two drawings independent of each other but with the same quota drawn each time—there will occur by chance a certain amount of overlap or agreement and a certain amount of nonoverlap or disagree-

TABLE 3.1   Extent of Decisional Agreement between the SAT-V Rule and the Actual Admissions Committee Decisions for the Randomly Sampled Group of Colleges, the High-Selectivity Group of Colleges, Harvard for 1960, and Harvard for 1964

Predictive Accuracy	Randomly Sampled Group			High-Selectivity Group			Harvard	
	MDN	1st Q	3rd Q	MDN	1st Q	3rd Q	1960	1964
ERROR-REDUCTION INDEX	40.4	33.8	47.7	31.4	26.3	35.9	37.3	13.6
% DECISIONS IN AGREEMENT	75.0	70.6	79.9	69.4	68.2	73.9	69.3	65.6
% ACCEPTANCES IN AGREEMENT	80.8	71.6	86.7	54.3	44.6	63.6	48.8	37.4

ment in the cases drawn. The error-reduction index indicates what proportion of the disagreement or error that would occur by chance has been eliminated by using the particular hypothetical strategy employed. In effect, this index expresses what degree of reduction in the probability of making a classification error has been achieved by basing the outcome predictions not just on knowledge of what quota a college accepts but also on the candidate data stipulated by the strategy. The error-reduction index is similar in concept to the "index of predictive association" developed by Goodman and Kruskal and described in Hays (1963).

More specifically, the error-reduction index works in the following manner.   The probability of making a prediction error before the hypothetical strategy is applied equals the probability of acceptance at a college (the proportion of its applicants a given college accepts) times the probability of rejection at that college (the proportion of its applicants rejected by that college) times 2. In other words, the resulting figure expresses the chance likelihood that the college actually will accept a candidate rejected by the strategy, and vice versa. It is the chance probability of disagreement between actual decisions and strategy-generated decisions. The degree to which this chance rate of error is reduced by applying a particular hypothetical strategy, in turn, equals the probability of making a prediction error before the strategy is applied minus the probability of making a prediction error after the strategy is applied (in other words, minus the proportion of the cases where disagreement was found between hypothetical strategy and actual outcome), divided by the probability of making a prediction error before the strategy is applied.

To illustrate the numerical meaning of the index, we give two examples. Suppose a college accepts half of its applicants. We then would expect to be in error 50 percent of the time if we based our predictions only upon knowledge of this quota (.5 acceptance probability times .5 rejection probability times 2). After applying our hypothetical strategy, however, suppose that now we make erroneous predictions for only 25 percent of the cases—that is, the instances of agreement between hypothetical strategy and actual outcomes constitute 75 percent of the total. Starting with a chance error level of .5, then, application of the strategy reduced the error level to .25, a difference of .25 which, when divided by the initial chance rate of .5, yields 50 percent as the degree of reduction in chance rate of error produced by application of the strategy (.5 initial error probability minus .25 final error probability equals .25, divided by .5 initial error probability equals .5 or 50 percent). The resultant error-reduction index of 50 percent means that, compared with the error rate from knowledge only of the accept-reject quotas, the reduction brought about by applying the strategy was one-half or 50 percent of the amount of theoretically possible reduction that could have taken place. This strategy thus offers a good approximation to decisional reality as compared to that found in our next example. Consider now a college that accepts 40 percent of its applicants and a strategy that yields correct predictions for 55 percent of the cases and hence errors for the remaining 45 percent. Under these circumstances, the chance error rate is 48 percent (.4 times .6 times 2), application of the strategy reduces this value to an error rate of 45 percent, and the error-reduction index is only 6 percent (.48 minus .45 equals .03, divided by .48 equals .06 or 6 percent). While an agreement level of 55 percent between strategy and actual outcomes looked reasonably good at first glance, it yielded only a 6 percent reduction in the error level expectable by chance at an institution accepting 4 out of 10 applicants.

How well did our hypothetical SAT-V strategy predict actual admissions decisions? We see from Table 3.1 that, for the median institution in the randomly chosen sample of 45 colleges, the SAT-V strategy reduces the chance error rate by 40.4 percent. It agrees with the admissions decisions that were actually made in 75 percent of the cases, and agrees with 80.8 percent of the acceptance decisions. At the first quartile institutions—those with higher selectivity—the SAT-V strategy was somewhat less accurate than at the median college; while at the third quartile institutions—those with lower selectivity—the SAT-V strategy was somewhat more accurate than at the median college. We view these outcomes as indicating that, despite the extreme simplicity of our SAT-V strategy, it provides a reasonably good approximation to the decisional reality.

Turning next to the national sample of 13 high-selectivity institutions, Table 3.1 indicates that the picture is generally similar to that for the first quartile or more selective colleges in the random sample. The error-reduction index value for the SAT-V strategy at the median high-selectivity institution is 31.4 percent, as compared with about 40 percent, as previously noted, for the median randomly chosen college. The median percentage of agreements between strategy and outcomes drops somewhat to 69.4 for the high-selectivity sample, and the median percentage of acceptances in agreement shows a distinct decline to 54.3. The fact that the high-selectivity colleges accept only a small portion of their applicants leads to a diminution in the number of opportunities for chance agreement on acceptances. If agreement on rejections were compared instead, the converse would be found—that is, the percentage of rejections in agreement would be lower for colleges in the random sample (which reject few candidates) than for colleges in the high-selectivity sample (which reject many). Given the small proportions of acceptances by the highly selective institutions, the error-reduction index (because it takes into account chance levels both of acceptances and rejections) offers a more accurate picture of the overall efficiency of the SAT-V strategy than does the percentage of acceptances in agreement. As we have seen, the error-reduction index value for the median high-selectivity institution is 31.4 percent. Given the considerable self-selection regarding SAT-V score levels for those who apply to the high-selectivity schools in the first place, it is noteworthy that application of our utterly simplistic SAT-V strategy succeeds in reducing the chance error rate by as much as it does.

Finally, we turn to the Harvard admissions data for the two years considered before—applicants for 1960 and for 1964 admission. Our previous interpretation would suggest that the SAT-V strategy should do a better job of accounting for admissions outcomes in 1960 than in 1964, and this is precisely what we find. As we see from Table 3.1, the percentage of all decisions in agreement between SAT-V strategy and actual outcomes declines somewhat for 1964 compared with 1960, the percentage of acceptances in agreement drops from almost half in 1960 to a bit over one-third in 1964, and the error-reduction index drops rather drastically from 37.3 percent in 1960 to 13.6 percent in 1964. Thus, while application of the SAT-V strategy reduced prediction error for 1960 by better than one-third, application of the same strategy reduced prediction error for 1964 by less than one-seventh. Clearly, the predictive power of our hypothetical SAT-V strategy at Harvard was greater in 1960 than in 1964, indicating an increase over that period in the degree of reliance placed upon student characteristics not associated with SAT-V scores when deciding upon admissions. The drop in our error-reduction index value resulting from application of the SAT-V strategy in 1964 compared to 1960 patently indicates that Harvard was indeed liberalizing its admissions policy over that period. In other words, it was depending less upon SAT-V scores and whatever other student characteristics co-vary with such scores. Harvard's appetite for verbal aptitude as a means for deciding whom to admit underwent a distinct decline. Recall, however, that this outcome is a rarity even when considering other high-selectivity colleges, and that our data for the high-selectivity sample concerned the same year—1964—as that for which we detected Harvard's de-emphasis of SAT-V scores.

To sum up what we have learned from Table 3.1, it is evident that a very elementary admissions-decision strategy—simply choosing in terms of SAT-V scores—reduces the chance error rate sufficiently to qualify as a reasonable approximation of what happens when actual decisions are made at the colleges. This dependence upon candidates' SAT-V scores in deciding on whom to admit is exhibited not only by a random sample of moderately to highly selective institutions, but also by a national sample of colleges confined to those that are highly selective and are choosing from applicant pools which, due to self-selection, are relatively high in verbal aptitude levels to start with. Using only the gross measure of a single personal characteristic—general intelligence—we have gone a good part of the way toward accounting for how admissions are decided. What would happen if we refined this measure of intelligence somewhat and also took into account academic achievement in high school—an accomplishment characteristic that is known to relate strongly to intelligence level? Consider this question in more detail.

While verbal aptitude constitutes a close approximation to the usual meaning of the intelligence concept, a better approximation would take into account not only a student's facility with words but also his facility with numbers—mathematical aptitude. It is no accident that the Scholastic Aptitude Test includes a mathematical as well as a verbal section in its attempt to assess a student's intelligence level. Given the substantial correlation between verbal and mathematical scores on the SAT, taking account of both should offer a more comprehensive sampling of the functions comprising the notion of general intelligence than taking account of either alone. So, too, we have noted that assessment of intelligence has been validated against the criterion of academic achievement—a characteristic that, while treated by the culture as a form of accomplishment, really is more appropriately understood as a promissory note for real-life accomplishment after schooling is over. And it is a note which is not as easy to redeem as one might have thought. When we consider academic achievement in high school as a factor in the acceptance or rejection of a college applicant, therefore, we are dealing once again with a characteristic that is closely tied to the intelligence concept rather than one which moves beyond it.

Given our considerable success in diagnosing admissions decisions on information about candidates' SAT-V scores alone, would we do even better if we utilized a more thorough estimate of intelligence—mathematical scores as well as verbal scores? And what if we also utilized information about academic standing in high school, since quality of grades is what intelligence tests are supposed to relate to anyway? To ask this question is to find out how much of the admissions picture can be understood by recourse only to one kind of traditional information—data about intelligence and about its academic achievement correlate. The more accurate our predictions turn out to be in terms of this limited set of information, the stronger will be the indication that very little outside this traditional and narrow information has room to play a role in the admissions process.

The aforementioned *Manual* did not contain sufficiently detailed material to enable us to pursue this matter for the national college samples already described, nor did Whitla's presentation of Harvard data contain enough detail for asking this kind of question. We did, however, have all necessary data for Duke University, one of the institutions that had been a member of the high-selectivity sample. Although mindful of the limitations attendant upon analyzing information from one institution only, we believe the results of this analysis to be representative of the admissions decision-making process in high-selectivity colleges generally, for Duke qualifies as an institution that is typical of those in the highly selective category. In the analysis where the hypothetical SAT-V strategy was applied to the high-selectivity sample of colleges, Duke as one college in that sample had an acceptance quota of 39 percent, as compared with a quite similar median value of 37 percent for the total sample of institutions. Given a selectivity level this close to what is found for the sample as a whole, it seems reasonable to explore the Duke data further as an aid to formulating our tentative view of the admissions decision-making process.

Our SAT-V strategy was extended in a very simple way in order to develop hypothetical strategies that would take into account the additional kinds of information that we have described, scores on the mathematics section of the SAT (SAT-M scores) and level of academic achievement in high school as well as SAT-V scores. High school academic achievement was defined by dividing the academic rank position of each candidate by the size of his class and converting to a standard score scale. Equipped with these data, we then formulated hypothetical policies that would utilize SAT-M scores and high school rank in the same manner as for SAT-V scores. Thus, the SAT-M strategy would rank the applicants in terms of their SAT-M scores and accept them in order of decreasing rank until Duke's acceptance quota was filled. The remaining candidates would be rejected. After computing separate results in this manner, we went on to develop analogous strategies utilizing each of the various possible combinations of the three measures in question as the basis for ranking candidates. There were four combinations in all: SAT-V plus SAT-M, SAT-V plus high school rank, SAT-M plus high school rank, and SAT-V plus SAT-M plus high school rank. The hypothetical strategy in each case was to add standard score transformations of the measures (standard scores making for equality of weighting) and then to rank the candidates in terms of the total of their standard scores on the two or three measures under consideration. Applicants once again were accepted in order of decreasing rank until the acceptance quota was filled, with the rest rejected. Thus, the formal simplicity of our SAT-V strategy was maintained in these further analyses. The difference was that SAT-M, high school rank, or an equally weighted sum of scores on two or all three of these intelligence test and grade quality assessors provided the basis for ranking candidates for admission in order of preference. Equal weighting constitutes, of course, the simplest assumption that could be made concerning how to combine measures.

The sample in our research consisted of all the applicants to Duke in 1966 for whom all three items of information just described—SAT-V score, SAT-M score, and high school rank—were available and who were not subsequently wait-listed. As no definitive action had been taken in the case of those candidates who were wait-listed, we thought it best to eliminate them from the analyses. In all, 4,270 applicants met these criteria, of whom 2,364 had been accepted for admission and the rest rejected.

The results of applying to these data each of the hypothetical strategies that we have described are presented in Table 3.2. Shown for every strategy is the percent agreement between the decisions made under the given strategy and the actual decisions made by the admissions committee, as well as the percent agreement between hypothetical strategy and actual committee regarding acceptances alone. Also shown for each strategy is the value obtained for the error-reduction index. The table contains entries for seven strategies—SAT-V, SAT-M, high school rank, and all of their equally weighted combinations.

What do these results indicate? First of all, note that application of the SAT-V strategy yielded agreement with the actual decisions for 72.9 percent of the cases, that 75.5 percent of the acceptances were in agreement, and that the error-reduction index yields a value of 45.1 percent or almost one-half. Why does the present use of the SAT-V strategy

TABLE 3.2   Extent of Decisional Agreement between Various Hypothetical Rules for Making Admissions Decisions and the Actual Admissions Committee Decisions at a Typical High-Selectivity College

Model	Rule	Error-Reduction Index	% Decisions in Agreement	% Acceptances in Agreement
1	SAT-V	45.1	72.9	75.5
2	SAT-M	48.5	74.6	77.0
3	High School Rank	47.9	74.3	76.8
4	1 + 2	56.6	78.5	80.6
5	1 + 3	58.2	79.3	81.3
6	2 + 3	60.6	80.6	82.4
7	1 + 2 + 3	64.3	82.4	84.1

result in even greater predictive power for it than was shown for the median institution in the high-selectivity sample considered before? Most likely because three-digit and hence exact SAT-V scores were available for the present analysis whereas in the previously described work we had to be satisfied with a more rough SAT-V score yardstick—scores grouped into 50-point intervals. In addition, elimination of the candidates who were wait-listed probably had the effect of removing those whose test scores were most borderline from the admissions committee's viewpoint, and hence most likely to elicit from us erroneous predictions.

Next, let us examine the results of applying our two other one-measure strategies—the SAT-M strategy and the academic-achievement strategy. For the SAT-M strategy, the percentage of correct predictions was 74.6, the percentage of acceptances in agreement was 77, and the error-reduction index value was 48.5 percent or again almost one-half. When in turn academic achievement constituted the single basis for ranking candidates, the agreement level with actual outcomes was 74.3 percent, the agreement level on acceptances alone was 76.8 percent, and the error-reduction index value was 47.9 percent—that is, still again almost one-half. Each of the three hypothetical strategies, based upon a variable taken singly, offered predictions of the actual admissions decisions that coincided almost 75 percent of the time with the actual admissions decisions, better than 75 percent of the time on acceptances, and reduced prediction error almost 50 percent.

Now let us turn to the results of using hypothetical strategies that base their predictions on various combinations of the indicators. Thus far we have considered these indicators one at a time. Continuing to study Table 3.2, we find that any combination of two variables is a better predictor than any single variable. Adding a second variable to the definition of a strategy improved the level of agreement between strategy and actual outcomes, whether for all decisions or for acceptances alone, by about 5 percent over that present for a strategy using only one variable. Also, the value of the error-reduction index climbed something on the order of an additional 10 to 15 percent. Combining all three variables into the "SAT-V plus SAT-M plus high school rank" strategy improved accuracy of prediction still further—to the level of 82.4 percent decisions in agreement and 84.1 percent acceptances in agreement. The error-reduction index in the case of this three-variable strategy was 64.3 percent—a gain of some 15 to 20 percentage points over the error reduction afforded by one-variable strategies.

Of particular interest in these findings is the stark contrast between the great simplicity, if not the downright crudeness, of our hypothetical admissions strategies and their marked success in predicting the actual decisions made. Taking account only of a two-part measure of general intelligence—SAT-V and SAT-M scores—and adding an index of high school grades, we find at a representative high-selectivity college that an admissions strategy accepting candidates in decreasing order of rank, on an equally weighted composite of these three pieces of information, correctly predicts 82.4 percent of all decisions and 84.1 percent of the accepted class. Application of this elementary strategy reduces the chance rate of error by almost two-thirds. Despite the fact that the college admissions process faces multitudinous variations in candidate characteristics, most of the decisions could be predicted simply by knowing each candidate's SAT scores and high school rank. Since intelligence assessment has been refined over the years in terms of its capacity for predicting grades, what we have found is that a tightly knit constellation of narrow and traditional data about the candidates accounts for most of the admissions outcomes. These results imply as well that use of the "SAT-V plus SAT-M plus high school rank" strategy, rather than a strategy based only on SAT-V scores, would have raised still further the degree of predictability of admissions decisions for the randomly sampled and high-selectivity groups of institutions in Table 3.1.

In evaluating the meaning of the error-reduction index that we have used to describe the predictive efficacy of our hypothetical strategies, there is a further point that needs to be made. When we refer to a strategy's predictive efficiency as reducing the chance error rate by a given percentage value, the implication is that a sufficiently good hypothetical strategy would yield 100 percent reduction of error or complete accuracy. This is true only in a theoretical sense, however. Actually the ceiling upon a hypothetical strategy's performance in measuring up against actual outcomes is undoubtedly lower. To claim 100 percent as the attainable ceiling for an error-reduction index is to assume perfect reliability for human judgment—admissions decisions—by the members of the admissions committees whose decisions we are predicting. In other words, we assume that the readers of the candidate files would make exactly the same accept-reject judgments if faced with the same pool of candidates a second time and if their memory of their previous decisions on these cases could be erased. This is, of course, a most unlikely assumption. Not all committee decisions would be made the same way twice, and hence we are dealing with a real-world situation where we cannot legitimately expect to account for 100 percent of a committee's actions. Let us consider in a bit more detail the bearing of this point upon the interpretation of the error-reduction index.

Suppose that an admissions committee in reading candidates' files would take the same action twice in 90 percent of the cases on two independent decision-making efforts, for each of which they accept half the candidates and reject the other half. Under these circumstances, the committee would reduce the chance rate of error in predicting its own decisions by only 80 percent, simply because 10 percent of the decisions made by the committee the first time would be different from the decisions they made concerning the same set of applicants the second time (.5, the probability of making a different decision the second time before rereading the files, minus .1, the probability of making a different decision the second time after rereading the files, equals .4, divided by .5, the initial probability, equals .8).

While we cannot actually determine the proportion of an applicant group about which there would be agreement by an admissions committee on two independent rounds of decision-making, we can evaluate the accuracy of our hypothetical strategies in the light of the very high probability that judgmental agreement would be less than perfect. This imperfect reliability of the decision-making which our strategies seek to predict, then, means that the error-reduction index values obtained as a result of applying these strategies represent a larger proportion of the achievable reduction than would be the case if the latter were 100 percent.

Conclusions

From the above evidence we have reached tentative conclusions that contrast markedly with the descriptions often given by colleges themselves of their admissions decision-making procedures. Despite the diversity of student characteristics that might be utilized in this process, and protestations to the effect that they are thus utilized, substantial proportions of the shots seem to be called on the basis of nothing more than an estimate of the candidate's general intelligence and of his grade quality in high school. These are characteristics which are interrelated because the evolution of intelligence assessment has, after all, been guided by the goal of predicting academic achievement. It is also the case that these are characteristics which in their upper range appear to have little bearing upon direct criteria of valued accomplishments. Yet intelligence test scores and grade quality within that upper range receive distinct emphasis when decisions about relative merit have to be made. Despite the pre-selection or self-selection for higher SAT scores and grades that takes place in defining those who apply to high-selectivity colleges, such institutions (as well as colleges of moderate selectivity) make heavy use of intelligence test scores and grade ranks in admissions. That this kind of use takes place, furthermore, seems to be insufficiently recognized.

Here is an illustration of the view typically held by high-selectivity colleges on what they are doing regarding admissions: ". . . as criteria have been developed to deal with the new pressures of larger numbers seeking admission, all the most selective colleges have opted for some diversity of talents, backgrounds, and career goals in their student bodies—and most of these colleges are choosing to seek a great deal of diversity . . ." (Glimp, 1967, p. 19). We confirm this view in our own analysis of the more recent of the two sets of data for Harvard, and Harvard is the institutional affiliation of the writer of the above passage, but we nevertheless find substantial dependence on academic skills as the indices for determining admissions in our study of a typical high-selectivity institution and in the national samples of colleges. We therefore must conclude that if regard for diverse forms of talent does enter into admissions decisions, it is only at a few institutions (such as Harvard), and not in the mainstream of the American admissions process or even at most highly selective colleges.

To repeat, we have thus far been concerned with documenting the status quo. The picture that has emerged shows, for most institutions and even most high-selectivity institutions, a considerable emphasis on intelligence test scores and grades in deciding whom to admit. But what is the alternative? What other ways of deciding on admissions could be put into practice? Before going further, we must discuss in more depth why it is particularly important to inquire into admissions criteria precisely in the case of institutions where competition for entrance is most severe—the highly selective colleges.

CHAPTER FOUR

Why Does It Matter Who Gains Access to the Highly Selective Colleges?

As the number of college-going opportunities available at minimally selective and moderately selective institutions of higher education increases, the sheer fact of college attendance per se is beginning to have little more meaning in our culture than did graduation from high school a generation ago. What matters, as far as access to more important roles within the society is concerned, is getting into the more prestigious colleges—that is, those in the high-selectivity category. These are the colleges with superior educational resources, where enrollment permits more meaningful learning and personal growth during the student's period of attendance. They are also the colleges from which a degree carries greater direct significance as a stamp of approval so that, merely by virtue of its possession, doors will open to occupational advancement.

The undeniable import of attending one of these high-selectivity colleges may be viewed, depending upon one's particular persuasions, as deriving more heavily from the former or the latter of the aforementioned two considerations—what Jencks and Riesman (1968) refer to respectively as "education" and "certification." There is little doubt that both considerations are valid as interpretations of the consequences of going to those colleges. Perhaps it is the case that, on the whole, psychologists will argue that the availability of a more stimulating learning environment is what matters more in these schools, while sociologists will tend to favor the idea that the significance of these schools derives more from their function of attaching to their graduates a label that possesses superior prestige in the eyes of the society.

By definition, entrance to the highly selective colleges is difficult: considerably larger numbers of students than can be accommodated seek their admission. This state of affairs must continue, for the basic reason that providing an educational milieu that ranks as superior is a very expensive matter. Quality institutions of higher learning therefore are not about to expand in a manner sufficient to meet demand; they do not have the funds that would permit such expansion, and spreading the available finances to cover more students would mean losing their status as superior institutions. Other institutions will seek new positions for themselves by traveling different routes from those available to their more selective peers and therefore will not fill the breach. However much attention the society may devote to education, an unprecedented reordering of its values would be required were it to deal with the problem of demand for college entrance by creating a sufficient supply of institutions offering the very highest calibre of faculties and facilities. Realistically, such an expectation would be out of the question even in a society that, unlike ours, was eager to make education its first national priority. But in the absence of this kind of availability, distinctions among institutions as to quality inevitably will be present, and in the wake of such distinctions there inevitably must follow greater pressure for admission to those institutions judged to be superior. Given the rate of population expansion in this country, there is every reason to expect that, if anything, the ratio of applicants to available spaces at the highly selective colleges will, despite increasing costs, continue to rise.

From the perspective of the colleges under discussion, the question becomes how they ought best to exercise their power of high selectivity. Selection inevitably will take place; but on what grounds? In the old days, various forms of ascriptive criteria held sway: wealth, place of origin, race, attendance at the "right" private high school. More recently, however, these colleges have come to reflect the society's increasingly meritocratic philosophy regarding the allocation of educational opportunities, and hence have sought to favor those applicants who seem to possess greater competence. This means those who are more worthy in terms of what they can do, regardless of the color of their skin, their residence, or their family's wealth. This brings us immediately, however, to the question of how best to understand the nature of talent. Of what does merit or competence consist? Colleges are now agreed in wanting to pursue essentially meritocratic standards of selection, so correctly interpreting just what are the extant forms of merit that human beings may exemplify becomes of paramount significance. Let us consider why this is so and then note how these colleges have tended to define talent.

If talents exist that are slighted by the more prestigious colleges, then students in whom such talents are represented will become less likely to exercise their proportionate influence upon the overall values and direction of the society. This kind of educational selection can then be said to constitute a societal analogue to one aspect of natural selection. It is analogous to the Darwinian idea that only those biological characteristics which receive adequate representation among breeding organisms will survive and flourish as generations go by. So too, whatever forms of human talent may be discriminated against in terms of access through the educational sorting system to socially influential roles will tend to drop out as the forms in question become increasingly under-represented among that society's value-makers. Whatever forms receive preferential treatment as far as educational opportunities are concerned, in turn, will tend to become increasingly emphasized in the society.

The particular exclusions and emphases that are systematically carried out regarding talents in the preferential selection of some students over others can, as a matter of fact, be viewed as a more potent instrument for influencing the society than whatever may be taught to the students who receive this special treatment. Jencks and Riesman (1968, p. 254) have made this point in relation to education for a specific profession, and it seems just as applicable to higher education in general:

> . . . it is easier to change a profession by recruiting new sorts of apprentices than by changing the rules of the apprenticeship. Professional schools have their students for only a few years, and they can do only so much with whatever raw material they get. But to the extent that they are over-applied and can select their raw material according to some preconceived plan, they can influence the profession they serve decisively.

In sum, how the highly selective colleges define talent, with its implications as to the kind of selection policy to pursue, seems to possess rather far-reaching cultural consequences.

Explicit focusing of research upon the process whereby students are selected for preferential access to the limited number of available superior educational opportunities, as distinct from and perhaps even as more important than the question of what particular form of pedagogical treatment may be provided to those who are selected, is a point of view that seems to meet with considerable resistance in our culture. Why does this idea of recognizing the importance of selection encounter such difficulty? Perhaps because it runs afoul of another strong societal value—egalitarianism. While the culture believes that preferential advancement should proceed on meritocratic bases, it also believes, somewhat inconsistently, to be sure, that all its members are essentially equal. If they are equal, then an educational institution should ideally be able to remake any raw material after applying innovative teaching techniques. As Ausubel (1968) has pointed out, the idea that any student can be formed into a creative contributor to society if the teaching he receives is sufficiently inspired finds at least one of its roots in ". . . the official environmentalistic bias of progressive education . . ." (p. 559). Such a doctrine of limitless human plasticity gives short shrift indeed to the role of competence differences among individuals; instead, the entire educative burden is placed upon the school.

The importance of who are the students attending the more prestigious colleges does not reside only in selective emphases and exclusions regarding what forms of excellence receive support toward influencing the value patterns of the culture. Besides whatever formal arrangements for instruction are present, the students who are brought together on a college campus learn from one another as well, and perhaps even more importantly. Most of a student's time is spent with his peers. If a college's admissions policies are prejudicial against certain forms of talent, then a student culture arises that minimizes the kind of implicit learning that can take place from exemplars of the talents in question. Viewed from the other angle, if the admissions approach adopted by a college is maximally consistent with the goal of representing among its students all the forms of talent that human beings display, the result will be a student culture that is maximally conducive to students' learning from each other. Having students on campus who are more representative of the actual range of talented human activities that exist in the world today means that there is more of value for them to absorb from one another; their informal interactions can be expected to yield a greater learning gain.

Students' learning as a function of interacting during four years in the same environment tends to receive little more than lip service when an educational institution sets forth its goals. Yet such learning goes on, usually affecting students at least as profoundly as the academic subject matter they must master. Jencks and Riesman (1968, p. 184) have pointed out the existence of considerable resistance against legitimizing the kind of implicit learning we have described:

> The habit of mind that equates education with attending lectures, covering reading lists, writing exams, and accumulating grades and credits is as firmly entrenched in the academic profession as among the students. The professional ethic dictates that "performance" is what really counts and that "what the students do outside the classroom is their own business." The dedicated professional scholar would be appalled by the idea of giving a student credit for spending his "leisure" on campus rather than at home, just as he would be appalled by a proposal to give tenure for hanging around the faculty club and making good conversation. Such scholars sometimes tell incoming freshmen that what happens outside the classroom is as important as what happens inside. But these same scholars bitterly oppose efforts to translate these sentiments into a system of grading.

So also, Jencks and Riesman note that no college offers more credit for a term spent living on campus than for a term spent commuting from home, while they suspect that the former yields more by way of meaningful growth for the student than the latter. Granting, then, that at least part of the significance of college derives from the educating that students provide for one another, the talents represented among the students on campus constitute a limiting factor concerning how much and what kinds of implicit learning can transpire.

We have spoken on the one hand of meritocracy and on the other of egalitarianism as educational ideologies that impinge upon how colleges view their responsibilities. As a matter of fact, it may well be the very presence of a general commitment to egalitarianism that makes the highly selective colleges all the more concerned these days with applying meritocratic standards when they are faced, as they inevitably are, with the requirement of admitting only a fraction of the students who apply. If they cannot admit everybody, at least they can choose fairly rather than on the basis of ascriptive characteristics such as religion, race, or family income. How does one choose fairly? The answer is by proceeding strictly in terms of the candidates' comparative merits.

Standardized tests of intelligence and high school grades appear to constitute, in our opinion, the basic means adopted by the highly selective colleges for implementing the wish to choose fairly. Of the two, furthermore, it is the intellective aptitude tests that seem to be favored, on the assumption that their universalistic significance offers a more accurate reading of genuine ability than is available in the form of academic grades. The latter, after all, may be influenced by teacher biases in favor of mere obedience and diligence. For this reason, commentators on higher education, such as Jencks and Riesman (1968), view the growing trend of colleges and graduate schools toward emphasizing intelligence tests more than grades as further evidence of the genuine pursuit of meritocracy and hence as maximally consistent with liberal democratic doctrine. To Jencks and Riesman, the use of grades over intelligence tests tends to constitute a pocket of resistance against fully meritocratic standards of evaluation because grading to some extent will reflect teachers' and school administrators' prejudices in contrast to actual talent. "The use of 'impersonal' national tests, on the other hand, frees the young from the control of those adults they see day by day, and makes the future depend more on the students' intrinsic qualities" (Jencks and Riesman, 1968, p. 64).

Note from the foregoing considerations that Jencks and Riesman are quite ready to assume that intelligence (as revealed by customary ability or aptitude tests) represents an appropriate definition of the kind of human merit in terms of which one should carry out preferential selection. Their view of talent seems to be that intelligence tells the story as far as college-relevant forms of intrinsic potential are concerned.

The rest of the picture is filled out in terms of motivational considerations, such as willingness to work hard and to conform to expectations.

That such a strong dependence has apparently developed on nationally normed tests of intelligence and on grades in screening applicants seems to be the result of many factors, of which the following three are surely among the most important: an increase in the tendency of colleges to view their own relative standing partly in terms of the average intelligence test score level of their students, the growth in recent years of the power of the faculty to determine admissions policies, and the increasing professionalization of the faculty itself. Consider each of these matters in turn.

Regarding the first factor, one comparative yardstick in terms of which colleges have come to view their status is the one provided by the intellective standing of their students. Admitting brighter students thus functions as a means of institutional image-enhancement: the higher the average intelligence-test performance level of the student body, the greater the prestige that accrues to the college. At the basis of such a practice is to be found, of course, the view that intelligence provides an adequate summary of student talent. The role of testing agencies in furthering the growth of this way of comparing institutions also deserves comment. Since their organizational goal is to maximize the use of and hence the degree of reliance upon the kinds of tests for which they have been tooled up to make items, testing agencies in their marketing work promote the tendency to define genuine talent in terms of these tests. As Mayer (1961) puts it, ". . . the test-makers, despite their pious remonstrances in conversation and in technical journals, have been pushing the schools ever harder to accept these instruments as expressions of a Larger Truth" (p. 376).

Regarding the second factor, faculty and alumni forces on college campuses have by and large tended to split along meritocratic versus ascriptive lines regarding which applicants should gain admission. Alumni have wanted their relatives admitted, and students from the geographic region of the institution favored, out of the feeling that a college really belongs to those to whom it has been most proximal. The faculty, on the other hand, has wanted to see criteria of academic competence applied and special interests put aside when it comes to deciding what students they should teach. The doctrine of meritocracy has gained sway in the larger culture, and the faculty has gained thereby greater power of moral suasion in making its demands concerning the kinds of students on whom it wants to spend its time.

It is evident, that in these battles between the faculty (with its commitment to meritocracy) and the alumni (with its commitment to the use of ascriptive criteria) in determining college admissions, the customary position is to view the faculty as representing a progressive stance. The faculty may, it is true, be progressive compared to the alumni. But focusing upon intelligence test scores and academic grade levels may not be the only route that could be taken for implementing meritocratic ideals. This would be a route reflecting the particular professional orientation that academicians adopt. The faculty, therefore, may not have a legitimate monopoly upon the force of moral authority that application of a meritocratic standard implies these days. They may in fact be reflecting their own one-sided interests in a manner not unsimilar to that which motivates the alumni, whose influence they customarily oppose. But this brings us to the last of the three factors already mentioned.

By the growing professionalization of college faculties we refer to the increased modeling of college instruction and grading on graduate school standards, where what matters most is the mastering of the conceptual content of an academic specialty. The faculty wants to treat the undergraduate as a junior edition of a graduate student, and this means selecting the former for admission in the same manner as the faculty has grown accustomed to selecting the latter, this is to say, in terms of apparent potential for becoming a scholar. We use the term "apparent" because we seriously question whether the customary admissions procedures for graduate school are really favoring those who are more likely to make insightful and perceptive contributions to scholarly fields, rather than those who are more likely to emphasize pedantry and conventionality in pursuing their work. Even in the academic arena itself, not to speak of the many domains of life that tend to be excluded from the purview of traditional scholarship, we wonder about the way in which human value is defined.

What in fact does get excluded from the academic professional's field of vision is worthy of further discussion, for the pattern of exclusion is not random but rather represents a systematic bias against certain modes of human activity. In a word, there is strong prejudice against practitioners. Academic professionals tend to give much more emphasis to studying art history than to being a painter, much more emphasis to working at literary criticism than to writing a novel, much more emphasis to musicology than to performing music, much more emphasis to studying a language than to being an actor, much more emphasis to studying political theory than to exercising political leadership. These academic professionals have themselves been selected for their work in terms of filters emphasizing theory more than practice, and vicarious experience more than direct experience. They have defined their professions accordingly. We can expect them, therefore, to apply the same kind of standards in making judgments about the kind of people they would prefer to have around as students. As professionals they view their primary pedagogical responsibility as recruiting others to become scholars like themselves— socializing others toward the pursuit of similar goals. They believe that academic grades assess scholarly talents, and they usually take this to be definitionally true. Intelligence test scores, in turn, predict academic achievement. Hence the faculty's interest in basing meritocratic distinctions upon intellective ability and grades. But what of those skills in which the faculty is relatively uninterested? Do such skills get slighted when basing college admissions on intelligence test scores and grades? If they do, then do we concur in the implication that they are less worthy of societal support than the skills which do receive emphasis?

Jencks and Riesman (1968) would like to see the definition of the academic guild system substantially broadened so as to include large numbers of practitioners on academic faculties. These would include writers being given equal academic status with scholars of English literature, artists being given equal academic status with specialists in the history of Greek vase painting, and politicians being given equal academic status with political scientists. For a similar type of recommendation, see Ackerman (1969). While the desirability of such broadening is unquestionable to anyone looking in from outside a given academic profession (and increasing pressures have been mounted in this direction), we cannot be very sanguine about how readily it will be achieved. The attempt requires us to fly in the face of the whole edifice of academic professionalism itself, with its well-established practices as to how one qualifies for guild membership and what sorts of activities are to be valued among members. To that extent, resistance can be expected.

Considerably easier to achieve, and in itself also conducive to broadening the faculty and the curriculum by bringing on to the campus more students receptive to these changes, would be a broadening in the range of talents represented among the students—if such broadening were found to make for differences in which students would gain admission in the first place. We have noted that whoever attends the highly selective colleges is a matter that carries consequences both in terms of the implicit education that students give one another and in terms of what sorts of students receive the aid that superior educational resources provide toward attaining greater influence in the society. Jencks and Riesman do not really seem acceptive to the idea of serious changes in student selection as a possibility; they have prejudged the issue of how talent ought to be defined—assuming, as we said earlier, that intelligence, as reflected in ability test scores, provides an answer that is sufficient psychologically. It is ironic that such foreclosure of the talent issue should occur at their hands, for they themselves have argued that educational institutions can exert greater effects through changes in admissions criteria than through changes in curricula. All that Jencks and Riesman would like to see, as far as admissions policies are concerned, is an even greater shift of emphasis away from grades and toward nationally standardized academic aptitude tests in deciding who is admitted. This is, of course, exactly the way the colleges appear to be headed. The fact is that, in terms of their conception of the nature of talent, Jencks and Riesman do not believe there is much that needs to be done at the admissions end of the picture. Before accepting such a conclusion, however, we feel that its underlying psychological assumption requires direct evaluation. Friedenberg (1970), in turn, sees the desirability of greater diversity in admissions criteria but seems insufficiently aware of the positive influence which such change—by bringing in more students who will support new kinds of offerings—then can exert on the broadening of curriculum and faculty.

By all means, then, let us move toward a broadened pedagogical setting. For example, let us see creative writers as well as literary critics enjoy equal academic standing and receive comparable representation in the English department; and let us award academic credit for writing novels, poetry, and plays as well as for skill at stylistic and historical analysis of literature that has been produced by others. In the art department, let us have artists and sculptors and potters, as well as specialists at the interpretation of art, and let us have studio courses where skill at producing works of art is fostered, receiving as much academic credit and available in as great abundance, as library courses where skill at interpreting the meaning of art is fostered. These are examples of the kinds of pedagogical changes that would be consistent with the goal of making the college experience more relevant to the rest of life, and the calls for relevance that one hears these days with increasing frequency start, in our estimation, from the awareness that academic professionalism has some serious shortcomings. But at the same time let us be sure that the admissions practices which determine student admission include sizable numbers who, for instance, are talented at creative writing, and sizable numbers who are talented at producing art objects—not just young persons whose main skills are in the domain of analyzing or interpreting the work of others. Changes along these lines in selection criteria—if the evidence turns out to suggest that such changes would cause differences in who is accepted by the institutions—would not only be easier to bring about than the kinds of pedagogical changes described, but would also support the attainment of pedagogical changes—because students most able to benefit from them would be on hand.

In a word, to those of a liberal persuasion, the trend toward an increasing emphasis upon meritocratic standards in contrast to ascribed characteristics as the means for deciding who shall receive greater educational advantages in the society—given an inevitable scarcity in the supply of superior educational resources, so that only some can receive advantaged treatment—must be greeted with approval. To be sure, a society in which ultimate status is fixed by the circumstances into which one is born may enjoy greater stability because everyone knows his place and cannot seek to change it. However, a society whose more talented members tend by reason of their ability to end up in positions of greater significance strikes liberals as a more just one and indeed as one which is likely to offer greater human fulfillment to a greater number of its members. The issue that calls for a close look, however, is what forms of human conduct should be considered more meritorious than others. What *should* we mean by such terms as talent, ability, or competence? To ask this question is to inquire about what constitutes an adequate psychological account concerning the nature of talent. It is to ask about what are the forms of merit that are available in college applicants for nourishment at the hands of the culture. In the next three chapters, we will examine the implications of this question for admissions practices at a representative high-selectivity college.

Status, Personal, and Accomplishment Characteristics of Those Who Applied and of Those Who Were Admitted

The results of our earlier analyses of college admissions decision making suggest that the moderately selective as well as most of the highly selective colleges rely heavily upon intelligence test scores and high school grades in deciding whom to admit and whom to reject. Against the backdrop of this finding recall that we began the book by considering the range and variety of student characteristics that *might* be considered as factors in the admissions process—provided that the information concerning these characteristics not only was obtained from candidates but also was utilized by those who make the admissions decisions. Our classification of student attributes assigned some to the rubric of status characteristics, others to that of personal characteristics, and still others to that of accomplishment characteristics. We noted further in considering these attributes that, to some extent and depending upon the aims and practices of each college, certain student characteristics in addition to grades and intelligence test scores of course do play a role in admissions. For instance, where a college gives preference to the children of its alumni or to home-state residents (both status characteristics), or where a college gives preference to applicants with an expressed interest in business or engineering (both personal characteristics), or where a college gives preference to applicants with demonstrated athletic ability (an accomplishment characteristic). The role of such additional factors seemed, however, to be a limited one.

Two broad generalizations can be derived from what we have set forth thus far. First, it is clear that the degree of emphasis given to any one characteristic in selecting a class of students from an applicant population has ramifications extending far beyond the characteristic in question. Since some characteristics are positively related while others are unrelated or even inversely related, when we give weight to a particular attribute in the sense that applicants are favored who possess it, we are also, by such a decisional act, affecting the relative weight assigned to other characteristics. The consequences depend, of course, on how the various attributes that describe the applicants are related. For example, SAT scores and high school grades tend to be positively correlated. If, therefore, an admissions committee chooses to emphasize the high school record and only admit candidates with high secondary school grades, the applicants who gain admission are likely to have high SAT scores as well. While SAT scores and high school record tend to co-vary positively, we assume that this will not be the case in considering the relationship between SAT scores and, for example, athletic ability. Here the linkage may be zero or even negative. Thus, if a college places heavy emphasis upon athletic prowess, consistently giving preference to applicants who were outstanding athletes during their high school years, the class invited to attend that college probably will be *different from* a class selected first and foremost for high intelligence test scores. Only if the students who excelled at athletics tended to be the same as those who excelled on the SAT—that is, only if these characteristics were positively related—would the same group of candidates be selected. Such examples are just the beginning. Needed for consideration is recognition of all the different kinds of musical instruments that might be called upon to play in the orchestra—all the attributes and their interrelationships that might play a role in admissions—so that we can understand the ways in which selection policies emphasizing one or more student characteristics influence the relative strength of *other* attributes in an admitted class.

A second generalization is that the preferences or biases expressed through an admissions process—the emphasis placed by a given admissions committee upon, say, high school record or non-whiteness or athletic ability or all three—constitute value judgments. Whether the bases for making admissions decisions are fully within awareness or relatively unconscious—and, given the paucity of research in this area, the likelihood is very small that the criteria for their decisions are completely known to the decision-makers—the fact is that the composition of the freshman class is influenced by the values of those deciding whom to admit. Evidence suggests that the greatest value seems to be placed upon intelligence test scores and high school grades in making these decisions. To the extent that these values are consciously maintained, they are held on the grounds that the two student characteristics in question are predictive of grade-getting level in college. But, given college courses as customarily defined, with their considerable limitations on the range of what is construed as appropriate academic fare, academic achievement in college may itself represent an overly narrow definition of the criterion that should be predicted. At least, we find ourselves confronting yet another value issue. Since collegiate education is presently at a point where curricula and grading systems, along with admissions policies, are faced with vociferous challenges, we must recognize that value judgments are at the core of the admissions decision-making process—judgments that greatly determine the characteristics of the students attending college and especially of those attending the highly selective colleges.

If emphases on particular characteristics reduce the degrees of freedom in considering other characteristics, and if these relative weightings in turn rest, consciously or unconsciously, upon value judgments, then we are under both a scientific and a social obligation to learn as much as possible about what are the options. Otherwise, values that we may wish to express, or values that for one reason or another we feel should be expressed, may not be reflected in our choices. Value judgments are inescapable; they will take the form of answering such questions as: To what degree should educational resources be devoted to the stimulation of nascent creative writers, of potential scientists, of those who do well at taking intelligence tests, of those with promise in the visual arts, of those from culturally disadvantaged backgrounds, of those with musical sensitivities, of those who are skillful at organizing business activities, of those who have received high grades in secondary school, of those with the ability to communicate eloquently through the movements of modern dance? Before we are in a position to make value judgments such as these with any degree of wisdom, however, we must understand the ways in which, and the extents to which, different weightings or emphases on various student characteristics impinge upon one another. If we admit more musicians, will the distribution of athletes be affected? How will acceptance of a larger number of culturally disadvantaged students affect interest in programs concerning the performing arts versus programs concerning history, political science, and economics? If we admit more potential scientists, does that necessarily mean admitting fewer potential novelists, essayists, and poets? If we permit more individuals with potential for artistic attainments to enter the freshman class, will we thereby reduce the SAT average for the class? In short, what effect does adding to the orchestra more players of different kinds of musical instruments have on the types and number of players of other musical instruments that can be included in the total ensemble? What alternatives are available for the kinds of orchestras that might be assembled? How do these different possible orchestras sound?

How can we learn what choosing mainly in terms of intelligence test scores does to the representation of talented nonacademic accomplishments in the class? Can we discover in what ways emphasizing the latter attainments as the basis for selection would affect the incidence of various types of status characteristics among the class membership? In sum, can we find out how the various characteristics represented in a class change as a function of the admissions policy exercised by the college? Given an applicant pool and a freshman class to admit, only one admissions policy—however multifaceted or simple, however consciously or unconsciously applied—can be exercised at a time. We can, on the other hand, offer various admissions policies that *might have been* applied in deciding whom to admit from a given applicant population and determine what *would have been* the resultant characteristics of the students accepted under each hypothetical policy. How much overlap would there be if we compare the class accepted under one hypothetical admissions policy with the class accepted under another such policy— with both hypothetical policies applied to the same starting population of applicants? How much overlap would we find between the class that was actually admitted and the class that might have been admitted had some particular hypothetical policy been in effect? The first question asks how different from or similar to each other are the classes that would result from applying different objectively described admissions criteria. The second question asks how closely do the outcomes of one or another hypothetical policy approximate the results of the admissions practices that were actually followed—with higher overlap meaning that the hypothetical strategy in question provides a relatively good account of how decisions actually were made and lower overlap meaning that the hypothetical strategy in question would lead to the admission of different students than were actually accepted. Both questions concern us in the research to which we now turn, along with a third: how do the classes that result from applying each hypothetical policy, as well as the class actually admitted, compare to the total applicant population in regard to various relevant characteristics? This third question indicates what sorts of emphases and de-emphases regarding particular attributes result from applying different admissions approaches to the total population of those seeking entrance.

Applicants to Duke University for the fall of 1967 received an application form containing an extensive array of inquiries. The questions concerned status, personal, and accomplishment characteristics, with the detailed questions and their requested replies set up in a manner that was standard for all candidates. The answers to the queries, together with other information, comprised a particularly rich set of assessment materials that were amenable to systematic analysis because of the form in which they had been collected. All this information was contained in each applicant's file to be studied by the admissions committee when deciding upon acceptances and rejections. The same information was used by us later in applying and determining the effects of various hypothetical admissions policies. In this manner it was possible for us to develop a social psychological account of the actual admissions process, reviewing its effects in terms of what the initial pool of applicants was like and in terms of what various alternative freshman classes admitted by one or another hypothetical decision strategy would have been like.

What we have done in essence is describe the total population of applicants to a typical high-selectivity institution in terms of a comprehensive assortment of status, personal, and accomplishment characteristics. We have gone on to describe in the same terms the subset of applicants who were actually admitted. And we then used the same characteristics once again to describe each of several subsets of applicants who would have been admitted if one or another of several hypothetical admissions policies had been followed. We applied four hypothetical policies: (1) maximizing SAT scores; (2) maximizing academic achievement in high school; (3) maximizing a combination of SAT scores and high school grades; and (4) maximizing the level of talented attainments displayed in various outside-of-school pursuits. Applying a hypothetical admissions policy to the applicant population involved exactly the same logic as the hypothetical decision rules that we used in the studies reported in Chapter 3—that is, all applicants were ranked from highest to lowest according to a desired criterion, such as SAT scores, and were accepted in decreasing order of rank until the absolute number accepted by the actual committee was also accepted under the hypothetical admissions policy. In our discussion we shall refer to the subset of applicants who were really accepted as the class admitted by the "actual committee." By contrast, those subsets of applicants who would have gained admission under one or another of the four hypothetical policies that we apply will be referred to as the classes admitted by the "SAT committee," the "high school rank committee," the "SAT plus high school rank committee," and the "nonacademic accomplishment committee." The dominating policy or bias governing the decisions of each of these hypothetical committees is self-evident.

In the remainder of this chapter we describe first our sources of data and procedures of data collection, defining the various status, personal, and accomplishment characteristics under consideration. Then we present and compare the characteristics of the total applicant population with those of the class admitted by the actual committee. In the two subsequent chapters, we shall point out the results of applying each of the four hypothetical admissions policies to the same population of applicants—dealing in Chapter 6 with the consequences of letting decisions be made by the "SAT committee," the "high school rank committee," and the "SAT plus high school rank committee," and in Chapter 7 with the effects of letting the "nonacademic accomplishment committee" make the decisions.

The Data

Our sources of data consisted mainly of the answers to uniform questions on the application forms, College Entrance Examination Board Scholastic Aptitude Test scores, and information about high school performance. These materials were requested of all applicants seeking admission to college in the fall of 1967. Materials that were sufficiently complete to work with and that could be handled without ambiguity by punch-card coding arrangements were obtained from the Admissions and Registration Offices for a total of 4774 applicants. This figure constitutes 90 percent of the 5309 applications reported in an independent count that year by the Admissions Office, and closely approximates the total applicant pool. We were, it should be mentioned, concerned with applicants to the regular liberal arts undergraduate program, and it is to this program that most students apply. Not under consideration were the relatively small number of applicants seeking enrollment in either of two professional programs that are also available to prospective undergraduates—a school of engineering and a school of nursing.

Our next step was to examine, for each of the 4774 applicants in the initial population, the admissions decision as reported by the Admissions Office. Our aim was to determine if the decision for each applicant could be classified unequivocally into an "accept" or "reject" category. Hence it can be seen that we conducted our work on records made at a point in time subsequent to the completion of actual admissions decisions for the class in question. These decisions were thus quite independent of any results obtained from our research. Of the 4774 applicants, we found that there were 168 for whom no clear outcome categorization could be made as of the time when the decisional data were compiled. Some of these 168 consisted of applicants who had withdrawn their files prior to the time when the committee was to make its decisions. Removing these 168 files from further consideration thus left us with a final applicant total of 4606. This last total constitutes the size of the applicant pool available to us for our research. Of the 4606 applicants, 2917 were men and 1689 were women. To permit study of replication across the sexes, results for males and females are reported separately in the data analyses that follow. Because of occasional deficiencies of specific items of information, the actual comparisons usually involve somewhat smaller totals of applicants and hence the precise totals available for any analysis are always recorded in the tables.

Consider now the definitions of status, personal, and accomplishment characteristics for which assessments were obtained from the applicant population. The attributes on which we gathered information were 26 in number: 8 of them status characteristics, 5, expressions of personal characteristics, and 13, descriptions of various kinds of accomplishments.

Status Characteristics

The following 8 items of information provided a picture of each candidate's social, economic, and cultural background.

Parent education   The application form requested the candidate to indicate the educational backgrounds of both parents. Parent education was defined in terms of the father's educational attainments if these were recorded. If not, then it was defined in terms of the educational level of the mother. We classified the responses according to the following system: non-high school graduate; high school graduate; post-high school work but no degree obtained; college graduate; and post-college work.

School type   From information about the high school attended, the candidate was classified as having graduated from a public, parochial, or private secondary school.

Type of home community   The applicant was asked to classify his residential environment as one of the following: a metropolitan area of over 1,000,000; a suburban region in a metropolitan area of under 1,000,000; a city of between 500,000 and 1,000,000; a city of between 100,000 and 500,000; a city of between 10,000 and 100,000; a town of under 10,000; and farm or open country.

Community economic resources   The candidate was requested to characterize the major economic resource of his home community as agriculture, heavy industry, light industry, residential, commerce, mining, or diversified.

Place of residence   The applicant's place of residence was categorized into one of four regions of increasing remoteness from the location of the university: home state (from North Carolina, the same state where the university is located); regional but not home state (from a southern state other than North Carolina); rest of United States (from a non-southern state, including Hawaii and Alaska); and foreign (from a foreign country).

Parent alumni status   If either the mother or the father of the applicant had attended Duke, whether graduating or not, the candidate was classified as having an alumni parent.

Financial aid   The applicant was asked to indicate if he was applying for financial aid. The distinction between affirmative and negative answers to this question was viewed as having relevance to the economic background of the applicant's family.

Race   Although nothing in the application materials asked the candidate directly about his race, the Admissions Office did identify all applicants who were known to be nonwhite. We used the information thus provided as the basis for categorization.

Personal Characteristics

Assessments were obtained concerning intellective ability, on the one hand, and the broad domain of interests, attitudes, and values, on the other. In all, five variables were defined.

SAT-V and SAT-M   The applicant was instructed to take the Scholastic Aptitude Test of the College Entrance Examination Board, and to have his scores reported to the university. This is, of course, a conventional manner of determining the general intellective ability level of the candidate for college admissions purposes. The test is divided into two parts—one assessing verbal ability (SAT-V) and the other assessing quantitative or mathematical ability (SAT-M). Scores are reported on a scale ranging from 200 to 800 for each part.

Some benchmarks for score interpretation are provided by considering the following data reported by the makers of the test (College Entrance Examination Board, 1968). For high school seniors in general, the mean score for males is 390 on the SAT-V and 422 on the SAT-M; for females, 393 on the SAT-V and 382 on the SAT-M. For high school seniors who go on to college, the mean score for males is 440 on the SAT-V and 509 on the SAT-M; for females, 467 on the SAT-V and 461 on the SAT-M. A candidate scoring 600 on the verbal section of the SAT exceeds about 95 percent of high school seniors in general and about 85 to 86 percent of high school seniors who enter college. An SAT-V score of 400, on the other hand, exceeds about 55 percent of high school seniors in general and about 32 percent of high school seniors who enter college. More detailed background information on score interpretation can be found in the aforementioned reference.

Terminal degree plans   The applicant was asked to indicate the highest academic degree he planned to obtain, with distinctions made among the following categories: B.A. or B.S., M.A. or M.S., B.D., L.L.B., M.D., and Ph.D. or Ed.D.

Proposed major   The applicant was requested to indicate his proposed major field of study in college. These proposed majors were classified by the Admissions Office into one of the following broad areas: humanities, social sciences, biological sciences, physical sciences (including mathematics), and other.

Career plans   The applicant was asked to indicate the general area of his career orientation, and his answer was assigned to one of the following categories: business, engineering, law, medicine, politics, science research, education, and other.

Accomplishment Characteristics

Of the 13 measures used for quantifying the accomplishment characteristics of the applicants, 2 reflected academic and the rest non-academic forms of attainments. We consider the former first.

NMSC recognition   On the basis of taking a test reflective of academic achievement and academic ability components, the National Merit Scholarship Corporation awards certificates of merit and letters of commendation to those earning sufficiently high scores. Students winning either of these forms of recognition were noted in the present category.

We have already discussed how quality of academic grades only ambiguously can be assigned to the rubric of accomplishment rather than personal characteristics. This is because in most instances academic grade-quality functions as a promissory note for expected real-world attainments rather than as a sign that the student has made an intrinsically valued contribution of some sort. The same point applies to earning a sufficiently high score on its test to gain a form of recognition from the National Merit Scholarship Corporation. While both grade achievement and NMSC recognition might more appropriately be viewed as personal characteristics, the culture tends to call them accomplishments, and for this reason we leave them grouped under the accomplishment label.

Converted class rank   As a summary indication of academic achievement, the candidate's secondary school reports his rank-in-class to the Admissions Office. This rank, expressed as a proportion in relation to the size of his class and transformed by a customary conversion to a scale ranging from 20 to 80, constituted our assessment of grade achievement in high school. The index does not consider any possible differences in high school quality. A score of 50 on this scale indicates that the student ranks at about the middle of his class in academic standing. A score of 60, in turn, indicates that he has exceeded about 85 percent of his classmates academically, while a score of 70 means that he has surpassed about 97.5 percent of his peers. Thus, higher scores on the 20 to 80 scale reflect stronger academic achievement. A more detailed explanation of this kind of academic achievement measure can be found in Wallach and Wing (1969).

Overall nonacademic accomplishments   The applicant was asked to describe his activities in each of seven areas of potential accomplishment outside the classroom: leadership, art, social service, literary activities, dramatic arts, music, and science. In each area, several statements describing forms of relevant activity were presented for consideration— the number of statements pertaining to given areas ranging from three to six depending on what seemed most appropriate in each case for adequate coverage. Statements concerning any area included descriptions of accomplishments commonly exhibited by students and descriptions of relatively rare accomplishments. The applicant was to check those that applied to him. Thus, for example, in the case of leadership, a commonly checked statement read as follows: "Participated as an active member of one or more student organizations." On the other hand, a relatively rarely checked statement was this one: "Elected president of student government or class." A total score for each of these seven areas was obtained by assigning values in the following manner for the number of statements checked by the candidate as descriptive of himself: 0 for no statements checked, 1 for 1 statement checked, 2 for 2 statements checked, and 3 for 3 or more statements checked. These scores were then added together to provide an index of overall nonacademic accomplishments. Since no area was represented by less than 3 statements and each score could range between 0 and 3, the various areas received equal weight in the final index, which therefore could range from 0 to 21. High scores on this index of overall nonacademic accomplishments indicate a breadth of attainment across areas as well as depth of attainment within areas. Low scores, on the other hand, indicate relative lack of involvement in nonacademic accomplishments as a whole, or the display of no more than relatively common accomplishments in the various areas. In brief, the index summarizes the student's generality of nonacademic accomplishments without referring to the particular area or areas involved. Further information about this kind of index and its construction can be found in Wallach and Wing (1969).

In our previous research, the type of index just described turned out to be unrelated to intelligence test results but was related instead to level of ideational output or ease of generating ideas (Wallach and Wing, 1969).

This kind of index seemed helpful as a means of learning something about the ideational resourcefulness of the student in the world outside the classroom.

The level of overall nonacademic accomplishments can be distinguished from the display of strong attainments within any one domain in particular, and it is to the latter issue that we turn in our remaining measures. With the assessments that follow we identified those individuals who had exhibited especially meritorious attainments in a particular line of nonacademic endeavor. Each of the seven areas already mentioned—leadership, art, social service, literary activities, dramatic arts, music, and science—was considered separately. A further distinction concerning literary activities also was made, with creative writing and editorial work viewed independently. Two additional areas beyond the seven listed before were assessed as well—athletic skills and the holding of a remunerative job. While these last two seemed to concern issues of a much less cognitive sort than the other seven areas, and for that reason were not included in the index of overall nonacademic accomplishments, athletics and employment seemed interesting in their own right as further indications of a student's activities beyond the classroom environment. The measures that follow thus concern 10 different lines of nonacademic activity. In the case of each measure, we were interested only in attainments that occur relatively infrequently and that indicate a high level of contribution within the area in question. Our objective thus was to insure that a relatively high criterion of quality within each area would have to be met. Scoring was carried out with no reference to the index of overall nonacademic accomplishments described before, although answers to some of the same questions provided the bases for assessment. Following are the queries which formed the assessment materials for each area.

Leadership   The applicant was identified as a leader if he indicated by checking the statement in question that he had been elected president of his student government or class.

Art   Categorized as an artist was the candidate who indicated by endorsing the appropriate statement that he had won a prize or an award in an art competition, or that he had entered an art competition.

Social service   The candidate was defined as a contributor in the social service realm if he indicated by checking the relevant statement that he had won an award or prize for work with a community or religious group such as a 4-H Club or a "Y" organization.

Writing   Identified as a creative writer was the applicant who indicated by checking the appropriate statement that original writing of his had been published in a public newspaper, magazine, or anthology (*not* a school publication), and/or that he had won a prize for creative writing.

Editing   The applicant was identified as an editor if he indicated by checking the appropriate statement that he had edited his school newspaper or yearbook.

Dramatic arts   Defined as a contributor in the area of dramatic arts was the candidate who indicated by his checking of statements that he had received an award for acting, playwriting, or some other phase of dramatic production, and/or that he had won an award in a state or regional speech or debating contest.

Music   The candidate was described as a musician if he indicated by appropriate checking of statements that he had won a prize or award in a musical competition, and/or that he had performed regularly as a professional musician, and/or that any music he had composed or arranged had received a professional performance.

Science   Described as a contributor in the field of science was the applicant who indicated by his checking of statements that he had won first, second, or third prize in a state or regional science contest, and/or that he had attended a summer science program sponsored by the National Science Foundation.

Athletics   The candidate was identified as an athlete if he indicated by checking the appropriate statement that he had won a district, regional, or state award in recognition for his athletic ability.

Employment   The applicant was defined as having held a remunerative job if he stated in answer to the relevant question that he had earned more than $500 during his last school year, including any summertime earnings.

The foregoing constitute, then, the status, personal, and accomplishment characteristics in terms of which the students applying for admission were described. We turn next to a comparison between the characteristics of the applicant population and the characteristics of the students who were accepted for admission by the actual committee.

The Actual Committee

Did the actual admissions committee value some applicant characteristics more than others in making its decisions? To answer this question, we took for each characteristic a test of the difference in strength or distributional pattern of that characteristic for the students accepted and the students rejected. To the degree that a given characteristic was more strongly represented in the accepted population than in the rejected population, or had a different distributional pattern in the former than in the latter, then the characteristic in question was one to which the committee gave weight—explicitly or implicitly—in arriving at its decisions.

Our means of examining statistically the difference on a given characteristic between the accepted and the rejected populations was a t test in the case of SAT-V scores, SAT-M scores, converted class ranks, and overall nonacademic accomplishments, and a Chi-square test in the case of all of the other characteristics. For the latter, distributions across categories for the accepted versus the rejected populations were at issue, as when, for example, we wanted to compare the frequencies of artists and nonartists in the accepted and rejected populations, or the frequencies of those with various proposed majors.

Table 5.1 shows the results of these tests, with a single asterisk indicating a difference between accepted and rejected populations significant beyond the .05 level of confidence, two asterisks, a difference significant beyond the .01 level, and three asterisks, a difference significant beyond the .001 level. Also found in Table 5.1 are descriptions of the strength or distributional pattern of each characteristic in the total applicant population and in the population accepted by the actual committee. Thus, while the statistical tests carried out compare accepted versus rejected populations, the descriptive material presented compares the total applicant population with the accepted population. The latter type of comparison seemed more meaningful for descriptive purposes because it permits the reader to see to what extent the accepted population deviates from the total population in regard to any characteristic under consideration. Where t tests are the statistic, means and standard deviations are presented for describing the data; where Chi-square tests are the statistic, the data are described in terms of the percentages of instances in particular categories. These points hold also for the analogous presentations that will appear in Chapters 6 and 7 concerning the effects of applying various hypothetical admissions policies to the same starting population.

What characteristics were emphasized by the actual committee in its work of selection? Consider status characteristics first, and recall that these were parent education, school type, type of home community,

TABLE 5.1   Characteristics of Total Applicant Population and
of Population Accepted by the Actual Committee

	Males		Females	
	Total Population	Accepted Population	Total Population	Accepted Population
PARENT EDUCATION (N)	2917	1231	1689	565
% Non-H.S. graduate	4.6	4.4	4.7	3.4**
% H.S. graduate	10.5	10.5	8.9	7.4
% Post-H.S., no degree	20.6	19.3	19.4	16.6
% College graduate	28.7	27.5	26.5	32.7
% Post-college	35.6	38.3	40.4	39.8
SCHOOL TYPE (N)	2912	1228	1681	563
% Public	72.3	77.3***	78.2	76.4
% Parochial	4.4	2.5	2.3	1.6
% Private	23.4	20.2	19.5	22.0
TYPE OF HOME COMMUNITY (N)	2915	1230	1685	565
% Metropolitan, > 1,000,000	16.0	16.1***	18.1	17.3
% Suburban, < 1,000,000	17.2	14.6	17.4	15.0
% City, 500,000–1,000,000	2.2	1.6	2.7	3.0
% City, 100,000–500,000	14.1	18.1	13.0	14.3
% City, 10,000–100,000	32.3	31.2	32.2	34.0
% Town, < 10,000	14.0	14.3	11.8	11.5
% Farm or open country	4.2	4.0	4.8	4.8
COMMUNITY ECONOMIC RESOURCES (N)	2913	1227	1686	565
% Agriculture	8.1	8.5***	6.3	5.1
% Heavy industry	7.7	7.0	8.7	9.0
% Light industry	10.2	11.2	11.2	11.9
% Residential	30.3	25.3	28.8	26.7
% Commerce	7.4	7.3	6.3	7.3
% Mining	0.5	0.4	0.6	0.7
% Diversified	35.8	40.3	38.1	39.3
PLACE OF RESIDENCE (N)	2915	1230	1688	565
% Home state	10.1	19.2***	12.9	22.8***
% Regional, not home state	37.9	39.6	39.9	36.6
% Rest of U.S.	50.6	39.9	44.8	38.2
% Foreign	1.4	1.3	2.4	2.3
PARENT ALUMNI STATUS (N)	2915	1230	1689	565
% Alumni	4.9	8.5***	7.1	11.7***
FINANCIAL AID (N)	2917	1231	1689	565
% Aid applicants	39.4	52.3***	41.4	51.0***
RACE (N)	2917	1231	1689	565
% Nonwhite	1.1	1.5	2.1	1.8
SAT-V (N)	2855	1230	1669	561
$\bar{X}$	593.25	642.00***	615.63	669.49***
SD	82.73	68.00	81.10	61.51
SAT-M (N)	2856	1230	1669	561
$\bar{X}$	635.00	674.90***	607.69	665.21***
SD	80.32	68.94	80.63	67.30
TERMINAL DEGREE PLANS (N)	2911	1231	1688	565
% BA, BS	13.1	8.7***	30.6	25.5*
% MA, MS	23.6	21.2	44.1	46.7
% BD	0.4	0.1	0.1	0.0
% LLB	14.1	13.2	2.3	2.1

TABLE 5.1   (Continued)

	Males		Females	
	Total Population	Accepted Population	Total Population	Accepted Population
% MD	22.8	23.2	9.2	9.4
% PhD, EdD	26.1	33.6	13.7	16.3
PROPOSED MAJOR (N)	2915	1230	1688	565
% Humanities	37.3	33.8***	53.6	54.5
% Social sciences	9.6	11.7	12.0	11.9
% Bio. sciences	25.6	26.6	17.2	14.2
% Physical sciences	27.2	27.5	17.0	19.5
% Other	0.3	0.4	0.2	0.0
CAREER PLANS (N)	2907	1228	1686	563
% Business	16.8	12.1***	5.7	4.3
% Engineering	1.4	1.6	0.2	0.0
% Law	18.9	17.7	2.7	2.3
% Medicine	23.9	23.9	10.7	10.1
% Politics	3.4	3.7	2.7	2.7
% Science research	14.0	18.6	13.0	15.3
% Education	6.7	7.6	26.0	24.3
% Other	15.0	15.0	38.9	41.0
NMSC RECOGNITION (N)	2917	1231	1689	565
% Recognized	26.2	47.4***	28.8	53.5***
CONVERTED CLASS RANK (N)	2755	1189	1592	544
$\bar{X}$	61.75	66.41***	65.50	69.92***
SD	8.07	6.62	7.50	6.31
OVERALL NONACADEMIC ACCOMPLISHMENTS (N)	2917	1231	1689	565
$\bar{X}$	8.32	9.12***	9.82	10.21***
SD	3.79	3.71	3.56	3.46
LEADERSHIP (N)	2917	1231	1689	565
% Leaders	17.3	19.3*	8.3	8.8
ART (N)	2917	1231	1689	565
% Artists	5.2	4.3	12.0	9.6*
SOCIAL SERVICE (N)	2917	1231	1689	565
% Social service involvement	20.1	20.9	19.8	20.5
WRITING (N)	2917	1231	1689	565
% Writers	9.4	13.2***	14.4	17.7***
EDITING (N)	2917	1231	1689	565
% Editors	12.8	16.2***	21.0	27.8***
DRAMATIC ARTS (N)	2917	1231	1689	565
% Dramatic arts involvement	7.4	9.5***	7.1	7.1
MUSIC (N)	2917	1231	1689	565
% Musicians	13.0	13.6	13.5	15.0
SCIENCE (N)	2917	1231	1689	565
% Science involvement	8.5	13.2***	7.0	9.4**
ATHLETICS (N)	2917	1231	1689	565
% Athletes	16.1	12.8***	5.1	4.6
EMPLOYMENT (N)	2917	1231	1689	565
% Employed	19.0	15.9***	4.7	3.4

NOTE: Here and in similar tables, asterisks for Chi-squares appear beside the first category of the characteristic in question. Such asterisks reflect significantly different distributions for accepted versus rejected populations across the full set of categories.

community economic resources, place of residence, parent alumni status, financial aid, and race. From Table 5.1 we find that only three of these status characteristics receive heavy and consistent emphasis for members of both sexes—place of residence, parent alumni status, and financial aid. Here and in all subsequent discussions of results as well, we concentrate on findings that meet the criterion of replicating at statistically significant levels for males and females. This approach thus gives us generalizations that apply to the selection process regardless of the candidate's sex. With regard to place of residence, candidates residing in the home state of the university clearly are favored over candidates coming from elsewhere: almost twice as large a percentage of home-state students are in the accepted population than there are in the total population for each sex. Similarly, applicants with parent alumni affiliations have an advantage over applicants lacking alumni ties. Distinctly higher proportions of students with alumni parents are accepted than their proportions in the applicant population for each sex. Turning to financial aid, we find that those requesting aid represent considerably higher percentages of the accepted population than of the applicant population for each sex. This last finding may mean that the committee is favoring the admission of students from less advantaged homes. While such an inference may be true to a degree, an alternative and perhaps more likely interpretation is that students who apply for financial aid tend to self-select themselves for high SAT scores and secondary school grade achievement because they believe that they would otherwise have no chance of receiving aid. As far as status characteristics are concerned, therefore, preference is given to home-state residents, those with alumni parents, and those who believe it appropriate to apply for financial aid. None of the other status characteristics receive much consistent selective attention. Of these other characteristics, we might note in particular that the proportions of nonwhites are about the same in the accepted population and in the total population for each sex—a finding that will be considered further in later chapters.

Let us now examine the role of the applicant's personal characteristics in the selection approach of the actual committee. At issue here were SAT-V scores, SAT-M scores, proposed major, and terminal degree and career plans. The SAT scores come first. It is evident from Table 5.1 that SAT-V and SAT-M scores play a pervasive role in the selection of candidates of both sexes. If we compare the average scores of the accepted population with the average scores of the total population for the members of each sex, we find score increments in the neighborhood of 50 points for each section of the test—the range for these increments is from about 40 to about 57 points. That these shifts toward higher scores in the accepted groups are considerable is evident when we note that the standard deviations in the applicant populations are in the neighborhood of

80 points, so that a rise of 50 points in the mean represents a change of something on the order of five-eighths of a standard deviation.

But where, viewed in national terms, were the applicant population score averages to start with? The applicant population score means for males were about 593 on the SAT-V and 635 on the SAT-M; for females, about 616 on the SAT-V and 608 on the SAT-M. The applicant groups themselves, therefore, already averaged in the region of 600 on each part of the test. Recall now the normative information presented earlier when we discussed the interpretation of SAT scores. We noted that means for high school seniors in general ranged from 382 to 422 for each part of the SAT, while means for high school seniors who go on to college ranged from 440 to 509 for each part. Thus, keeping in mind that standard deviations for the applicant groups were about 80, there were practically no candidates who scored below the means for high school seniors in general, and only a few candidates who scored below the means for high school seniors who go on to college. It is evident by these yardsticks that the applicants are highly preselected or self-selected to begin with in terms of SAT scores. When the admissions committee discriminates among these applicants in terms of their SAT scores anyway, it must draw fine lines—lines whose meaning may be questionable. By SAT standards most of the applicants are well qualified. Yet even within this top half of the SAT-score range for college-going high school seniors, the committee based its selections in part upon the principle that the higher the SAT score, the more acceptable the candidate.

Turning to personal characteristics reflecting interests, attitudes, and values, the only consistent and systematic effect for both sexes concerns the role of terminal degree plans. In the case of males and females, the committee tended to prefer candidates who expressed intentions of going on for a doctorate and tended to underselect candidates who planned to terminate their formal education at the bachelor's degree level. This suggests an inclination on the committee's part to favor applicants whose interests and plans have a scholarly orientation.

Regarding accomplishment characteristics, consider first the two indicators of attainments in the academic sphere—NMSC recognition and converted class rank. Both exerted strong and consistent influences on the committee's actions in the case of members of both sexes. As far as recognition by the National Merit Scholarship Corporation is concerned, the percentages of students so recognized come close to being twice as high in the accepted group as in the applicant group for each sex. These proportions rise to the neighborhood of one-half in the accepted groups, compared to something like one-quarter or three-tenths in the applicant groups. This is not surprising in view of the weight attached to SAT scores in the decision-making process, for the tests administered by the NMSC are similar in large part to the SAT.

What about high school grade quality? The picture is one of strong and consistent emphasis on grade achievement for applicants of both sexes in the selection decisions made. Starting from mean score levels that already are better than 60 in the applicant population of each sex (thus signifying, as we said before in describing the converted class rank measure, that the average applicant exceeds about 85 percent of his classmates in grade quality) the accepted groups rank still higher yet in their grades. On the converted class rank measure, the mean of those accepted is about 3.5 to 4.5 scale units higher than the mean of the students who were applying. This is a considerable increase because it represents a change of about one-half of a standard deviation, as measured in terms of the standard deviation for the total applicant population of each sex. Again, this is no surprise in view of the emphasis placed on higher SAT scores in the accepted groups because of the substantial relationship between SAT scores and high school grades.

Finally, let us take a look at nonacademic attainments, considering first the index which reflected the candidate's generality of nonacademic accomplishments across the areas of leadership, art, social service, literary activities, dramatic arts, music, and science. The accepted population is higher than the total population on this index in the case of both sexes. It should be noted, however, that this rise for each sex is much smaller in relation to the standard deviations for the respective applicant populations than are the effects for SAT scores and converted class rank. For overall nonacademic accomplishments, the increments are on the order of one-fifth of a standard deviation for the males and one-ninth of a standard deviation for the females. By comparison, the mean increments for accepted populations over applicant populations were about five-eights of a standard deviation for SAT scores and about one-half a standard deviation for converted class rank. While some emphasis thus seems to be given to overall nonacademic accomplishments in the selection process, the degree of emphasis is substantively minor when compared to the weight given to SAT scores and high school grade quality. Now we consider the findings concerning students who show particularly meritorious nonacademic attainments in a given area.

From the results shown in Table 5.1 it is evident that selection effects favoring applicants with strong nonacademic attainments in these areas are modest at best. They are found, consistently for both sexes, only in the case of writers, editors, and those with science involvement—three of the ten areas assessed. For the remaining seven areas, the picture is one of no effect for both sexes (those with social service involvement and musicians), no effect for one sex and only a small positive effect for the other (leaders and those with dramatic arts involvement), or no effect for one sex and actually a *negative* selection effect for the other (artists, athletes, and those who were employed). Thus we have to infer that little by way of positive selection weight is given to strong nonacademic attainments except in the fields of writing, editing, and science. How much more attention could be given to accomplishments even in these realms will concern us later. Bear in mind that these fields, with their emphasis on words and numbers, stand closest to the modes of inquiry that traditionally occupy a central place in higher educational curricula. Among the other areas of potential nonacademic attainments are ones, such as art, music, and drama, that may well be viewed as making equally important contributions to human knowledge, and as offering equally deep insights into the unique properties of the human condition. These attainments, however, traditionally have tended to be looked upon as relatively frivolous, peripheral, or incidental.

To sum up our findings so far: First, it is clear that considerable weight attaches to SAT-V scores, SAT-M scores, and academic standing in high school. Another characteristic (the assessment of which is unquestionably linked with those just considered) is recognition by NMSC, and it too received considerable weight. Still another characteristic (and one that likely is interrelated with intelligence test scores and high school rank) that received emphasis is application for financial aid. It seems likely that only applicants with very impressive academic credentials tend to believe they have a chance of receiving such aid if they ask for it. Therefore the cluster of student characteristics just considered seems to center upon the committee's value preference favoring admission of those candidates who are conventionally marked as most highly qualified in academic terms. Emphasis on two other characteristics suggests the operation of another value preference—the tendency to favor the home team in some degree. This would seem to be an appropriate interpretation for the evidence indicating higher acceptance rates for applicants from the home state of the university and for applicants whose mothers or fathers were alumni. And finally, relatively minor but consistent inclinations were found to favor applicants with higher levels of overall nonacademic accomplishments, particularly those with nonacademic attainments in literature and science.

These, then, are the salient features of the selection effects exercised by an actual admissions committee at a typical high selectivity institution. Strong emphasis in deciding whom to accept is given to conventional academic qualifications, some emphasis also is given to whether the applicant is from the university's region or from a university-affiliated family, and again some emphasis is given to demonstrated nonacademic accomplishments. With these findings serving as a benchmark, we turn now to an exploration of what the characteristics of the admitted class *might have been* if different alternative hypothetical admissions policies had been exercised in relation to the same initial pool of applicants.

CHAPTER SIX

Three Hypothetical Classes Selected for Academic Skills: What They Are Like and How They Compare with the Class Actually Accepted

Having examined the status, personal, and accomplishment characteristics of students selected by the actual admissions committee, we now explore the hypothetical. In this chapter we ask how policies maximizing one or another of several definitions of academic talent would compare with each other and with what is actually done. In the next chapter we will consider what would happen under a policy maximizing talented attainments outside the classroom.

We have assessed the effects of the actual committee's selection practices by comparing the characteristics of students accepted for admission with the characteristics found in the total population of applicants. To the degree that a given attribute was more strongly represented in the accepted population than in the applicant pool, or showed a different distribution in the former than in the latter, we inferred that the characteristic in question was one to which the committee gave weight—explicitly or implicitly—in arriving at its decision. Now we want to carry out the same kind of assessment for hypothetical committees that are making their decisions purely and simply in terms of a specific guideline based on the maximizing of academic skills in the class chosen for admission. Three such guidelines will concern us: one that considers only a candidate's SAT scores, one that considers only his high school grades, and one that considers a combination of both. The questions we ask thus take the following form: How does an admissions policy framed purely in terms of accepting students with the highest available SAT scores affect the characteristics of the admitted class? How does a policy based solely on accepting students with the highest available high school grades affect the characteristics of the admitted class? And finally, how does a policy based entirely on a combined consideration of SAT scores and high school grades affect the characteristics of the admitted class?

But beyond this first inquiry, which parallels for these hypothetical policies the kind of question raised in the preceding chapter for the practices of the actual committee, there are other important matters to explore as well. We know from the findings in Chapter 3 that there is bound to be substantial overlap between what the actual committee does and the effects of hypothetical committees whose decisions are predicated upon SAT scores, high school grades, or both. That is to say, we expect to find that a sizable majority of the applicants selected for entrance by the actual committee will be the same as those selected by a hypothetical committee so conceived—although of course we shall want to document this point. Yet there will be differences. We have already seen that the actual committee favors—whether by intention or not—*some* characteristics in addition to high SAT scores and grades. Alumni affiliation is, for instance, a characteristic found in a greater percentage of admitted applicants than rejected ones. Would a hypothetical committee that adheres strictly to a policy of preferring students with the highest SAT scores also favor students with alumni connections? To put the issue another way, is alumni affiliation a factor that happens to vary concomitantly with SAT scores, so that to select students with high SAT's is inevitably to increase also the proportion of alumni children? Or does the actual committee give preference to alumni children *as distinct from* its preference for those with high SAT scores?

What we wish to determine is a picture of what else besides academic proficiency and its correlates the actual committee values. When a hypothetical committee, selecting a class in such a way as to maximize one or another measure of academic skills, differs with the decisions made by the actual committee, what is the nature of those differences? Suppose we take SAT scores as the index of academic skills under consideration. The question might then be phrased: When the actual committee admits some candidates with lower SAT scores than the SAT scores of other candidates available in the applicant pool—that is, when the actual committee admits candidates rejected by the SAT committee for insufficiently high SAT scores—what are those candidate characteristics that the actual committee finds sufficiently valuable to warrant admission? What characteristics does the actual committee value strongly besides those indicating or related to high intelligence?

Our approach to these matters was to "admit" from the same total applicant population three successive hypothetical classes, each based entirely on maximizing a particular definition of academic skills. The first of these hypothetical classes consisted of the applicants admitted by our "SAT Committee"—a decision rule ignoring everything about the candidates except their SAT scores. The second hypothetical class consisted of the applicants admitted by our "High School Rank Committee"—a decision rule considering only the candidate's high school grades. The third hypothetical class consisted of those applicants admitted by our "SAT plus High School Rank Committee"—a decision rule considering a weighted combination of the student's SAT scores and academic rank in high school. To arrive at the groups accepted and rejected by each hypothetical committee, our procedure, as described before, was quite simple. We ranked all candidates from highest to lowest on the basis of the selection criterion used by the given "committee," and then accepted in order from the highest rank down until reaching the limit set by the acceptance quota as defined by the actual number of applicants that had been selected. The rest were rejected. In the event of a tie or ties at the lowest-ranking accept position, we chose candidates from the tied ranks at random until we had filled the quota.

For each of these classes in turn, we asked the following questions. First, how much overlap or correspondence is there between the decisions made by the actual committee and by the given hypothetical committee—or, to what extent are their admissions decisions in agreement? Second, when we exercise each of the given hypothetical policies, what are the resultant characteristics of the admitted class? Again, as in the last chapter, our descriptive material for answering this question compares the accepted population against the yardstick of the total applicant population, while the statistical tests contrast accepted versus rejected populations. This second question could be rephrased to ask, how does a selection policy based exclusively on SAT scores, or on high school grades, or on both, shape the status, personal, and accomplishment characteristics of those admitted? Third, what are the characteristics that differentiate the two groups of applicants about whom the actual committee and the given hypothetical committee made opposing decisions—the applicants accepted by the actual committee but rejected by the hypothetical committee as compared with the applicants rejected by the actual committee but accepted by the hypothetical committee? The answers to this last question tell us what else counts for the actual committee besides academic proficiency and its correlates.

The SAT Committee

This hypothetical committee recognizes the intelligence test scores of the candidates as the only human attribute it wishes to take into account. For reasons already considered, we can expect such an approach to represent at least to some degree a part of the real world of college admissions. Thus, as discussed in Chapter 4, emphasis by an admissions committee on high intelligence test scores comes about in part as a result of attempts by colleges to compare themselves with one another. It is common for institutions of higher education to view their relative worth to some extent in terms of the SAT scores earned by their student bodies—those colleges boasting higher test scores rating higher in the pecking order than the others. As a result some colleges compete with one another for institutional prestige by attempting through their admissions practices to raise the SAT score level of their students. Note too that SAT scores may be weighted heavily by admissions committees because these test scores constitute a nationally normed index: they are numbers assigned on a nationwide basis. Hence it is felt that such scores are inherently more reliable and fair in assessing the worthiness of applicants than measures developed at a local community level or in school settings. Many college faculty members and administrators may, moreover, perceive scores on nationally standardized tests as the most valid means of assessing genuine intelligence. In turn, they take intelligence as reflecting competence in general. What, then, would be the effects of choosing only in terms of SAT scores? To provide a single SAT index for each candidate, standard scored and hence equally weighted transformations of the SAT-V and SAT-M scores were summed. The acceptance quota for each sex was then filled by admitting candidates from the highest rank down on the basis of the combined SAT scores.

Let us first examine the degree of overlap between the classes selected by the actual committee and by the SAT committee, as set forth in Table 6.1. Here and in later tables of the same form we present several ways of viewing the overlap or correspondence between one admissions approach and another. The upper part of the table compares the admissions actions taken by the actual committee and the SAT committee by presenting the observed frequencies of agreement and disagreement between the two. Entries for agreement consist of all cases where both committees accept or reject a candidate. Entries for disagreement consist of all cases where the two committees take noncongruent actions—one accepts and the other rejects. Frequencies expected on the basis of chance for the various categories also are given. These expected frequencies were computed by multiplying the probability of an applicant's acceptance (or rejection) by one committee times the probability of acceptance (or rejection) by the other. The numbers are set by the known proportions of candidates accepted and rejected in actuality. For instance, the probability of acceptance of a female applicant by the actual committee is .344. The probability of her acceptance by the SAT committee also must be .344, because the admissions quota for the SAT committee is determined by the number actually admitted. We multiplied .344 times .344 to obtain .118 as the proportion of the total number of female applicants (1573) which we would expect the two committees to agree in accepting by mere chance, thus yielding a chance expected frequency of 186 acceptances for females. That is to say, on the basis of chance selection alone, if there were nothing systematic going on to bring about greater or lesser agreement, we would expect the two committees to accept 186 females that were the same merely because both committees had to select 34.4 percent of the applicant pool.

It is apparent from the upper part of Table 6.1 that the number of cases of agreement between the actual and the SAT committees (the accept-accept and reject-reject cells) far exceeds what would be expected by chance, and the number of cases of disagreement between the two (the accept-reject and reject-accept cells) is much smaller than the chance expectancy. The lower part of the table summarizes these findings on predictive accuracy by presenting numerical values for three measures: the error-reduction index, whose computation and interpretation were discussed in Chapter 3; the percentage of all decisions

TABLE 6.1   Extent of Decisional Agreement between the Actual Committee and the SAT Committee

| | SAT Committee Admissions Decisions | | | | | |
| | Males | | | Females | | |
Actual Committee Admissions Decisions	Accept	Reject	Total Observed	Accept	Reject	Total Observed
Accept { Observed	856	332	1188	358	183	541
Accept { Expected	522	666		186	355	
Reject { Observed	332	1185	1517	183	849	1032
Reject { Expected	666	851		355	677	
Total observed			2705			1573

Predictive Accuracy	Males	Females
Error-reduction index	50.2	48.5
% Decisions in agreement	75.5	76.7
% Acceptances in agreement	72.1	66.2

NOTE: Applicants lacking SAT scores or converted class rank scores have been excluded from the analyses in Tables 6.1, 6.4, 6.7, and 6.9.

(acceptances and rejections) on which the two committees were in agreement; and the percentage of acceptances on which they were in agreement. These measures indicate considerable correspondence between the SAT committee and the actual committee. The error-reduction index percentages of 50.2 for the males and 48.5 for the females tell us that the decisions of SAT and actual committees overlap with one another sufficiently to reduce the chance rate of error by about one-half. In fact, fully three quarters of the decisions made by the SAT committee are the same as those of the actual committee—75.5 percent of all decisions on males and 76.7 percent of all decisions on females. Looking only at acceptances, the SAT committee would have ended up with 72.1 percent of the men and 66.2 percent of the women admitted by the actual committee: proportions far larger than those expected on the basis of chance.

What, then, are the characteristics of this SAT class? Table 6.2 does for the SAT class what Table 5.1 in the last chapter did for the actual class: it describes the attributes of the accepted population against the backdrop of the attributes of the total population of applicants. And in what ways does the SAT-selected class differ from the actual class? Table 6.3 focuses on the differences between the SAT class and the actual class by contrasting for each characteristic the candidates accepted by the SAT committee but rejected by the actual committee with the candidates accepted by the actual committee but rejected by the SAT committee. In the following pages, we consider the various status, personal, and accomplishment characteristics of the students in the light of both kinds of questions.

Let us turn first to the status characteristics. Table 6.2 shows that there are statistically significant selection effects consistent for both sexes in the case of educational background of parents, request for financial aid, and race of applicant. The SAT committee admits smaller proportions of candidates from home backgrounds where there are no college degrees, and larger proportions from families with college degrees or postcollege education. As to race, the SAT committee rejects almost all nonwhite candidates. In fact, only one nonwhite candidate, a female, is admitted by the SAT committee. For these two status characteristics, then, the SAT committee plays the role of restricting admission of students from what might be called culturally disadvantaged backgrounds. Financial aid applicants, however, are favored by the SAT committee. We suspect that this last bias appears not because SAT-based selection favors those needing financial aid but because those who apply for financial aid have a tendency to select themselves for high SAT scores.

What about the status characteristics of those applicants about whom the SAT committee and the actual committee made opposing decisions? We find that there are no consistent statistically significant differences

TABLE 6.2   Characteristics of Total Applicant Population
and of Population Accepted by the SAT Committee

	Males		Females	
	Total Population	Accepted Population	Total Population	Accepted Population
PARENT EDUCATION (N)	2855	1230	1669	561
% Non-H.S. graduate	4.3	3.2**	4.8	3.6*
% H.S. graduate	10.5	9.3	8.9	7.3
% Post-H.S., no degree	20.4	19.6	19.2	17.5
% College graduate	28.8	29.9	26.6	32.3
% Post-college	36.0	38.0	40.6	39.4
SCHOOL TYPE (N)	2850	1228	1661	557
% Public	72.1	74.3*	78.1	77.4
% Parochial	4.3	3.4	2.3	2.3
% Private	23.6	22.3	19.5	20.3
TYPE OF HOME COMMUNITY (N)	2853	1229	1665	561
% Metropolitan, > 1,000,000	15.8	18.9***	18.1	21.0
% Suburban, < 1,000,000	17.3	18.3	17.3	18.0
% City, 500,000–1,000,000	2.2	1.9	2.8	2.3
% City, 100,000–500,000	14.1	15.1	12.9	10.5
% City, 10,000–100,000	32.4	30.0	32.4	31.0
% Town, < 10,000	13.9	12.6	11.8	12.1
% Farm or open country	4.3	3.2	4.7	5.0
COMMUNITY ECONOMIC RESOURCES (N)	2851	1226	1666	561
% Agriculture	8.1	6.1***	6.4	5.3
% Heavy industry	7.6	6.9	8.6	7.5
% Light industry	10.1	8.1	11.3	11.1
% Residential	30.3	32.8	28.8	31.0
% Commerce	7.6	8.1	6.3	6.6
% Mining	0.5	0.2	0.6	0.5
% Diversified	35.8	37.8	38.0	38.0
PLACE OF RESIDENCE (N)	2854	1229	1668	561
% Home state	10.3	8.4*	13.1	12.7
% Regional, not home state	38.0	40.2	39.6	38.7
% Rest of U.S.	50.3	50.2	44.9	47.2
% Foreign	1.4	1.2	2.4	1.4
PARENT ALUMNI STATUS (N)	2854	1229	1669	561
% Alumni	5.0	4.1	7.1	5.5
FINANCIAL AID (N)	2855	1230	1669	561
% Aid applicants	39.2	48.3***	41.6	50.8***
RACE (N)	2855	1230	1669	561
% Nonwhite	1.0	0.0***	2.0	0.2***
SAT-V (N)	2855	1230	1669	561
$\bar{X}$	593.25	659.66***	615.63	688.71***
SD	82.73	53.82	81.10	46.34

TABLE 6.2 (Continued)

	Males		Females	
	Total Population	Accepted Population	Total Population	Accepted Population
SAT-M (N)	2855	1230	1669	561
$\bar{X}$	634.99	698.27***	607.69	680.26***
SD	80.34	49.37	80.63	47.40
TERMINAL DEGREE PLANS (N)	2849	1229	1668	560
% BA, BS	12.8	8.5***	30.5	23.2***
% MA, MS	23.8	22.5	44.2	47.4
% BD	0.4	0.2	0.1	0.0
% LLB	14.0	14.1	2.3	2.7
% MD	22.8	20.1	9.2	10.0
% PhD, EdD	26.2	34.7	13.7	16.8
PROPOSED MAJOR (N)	2854	1229	1668	560
% Humanities	37.1	35.1***	53.7	49.3*
% Social sciences	9.8	12.2	12.0	13.4
% Bio. sciences	25.5	23.8	17.1	16.3
% Physical sciences	27.3	28.7	17.0	20.9
% Other	0.3	0.2	0.2	0.2
CAREER PLANS (N)	2846	1228	1666	560
% Business	16.9	13.3***	5.8	3.9***
% Engineering	1.4	1.5	0.2	0.2
% Law	18.8	18.6	2.7	2.9
% Medicine	23.8	21.3	10.7	10.5
% Politics	3.4	3.8	2.7	2.1
% Science research	14.2	18.7	13.1	16.3
% Education	6.6	8.4	25.6	19.3
% Other	14.9	14.4	39.1	44.8
NMSC RECOGNITION (N)	2855	1230	1669	561
% Recognized	26.4	53.0***	28.9	59.7***
CONVERTED CLASS RANK (N)	2705	1181	1573	543
$\bar{X}$	61.88	64.52***	65.50	68.05***
SD	8.01	7.68	7.48	6.92
OVERALL NONACADEMIC ACCOMPLISHMENTS (N)	2855	1230	1669	561
$\bar{X}$	8.33	8.76***	9.81	10.04
SD	3.78	3.68	3.56	3.55
LEADERSHIP (N)	2855	1230	1669	561
% Leaders	17.2	17.7	8.3	8.0
ART (N)	2855	1230	1669	561
% Artists	5.2	4.1*	11.9	10.5
SOCIAL SERVICE (N)	2855	1230	1669	561
% Social service involvement	20.0	19.4	19.9	18.7
WRITING (N)	2855	1230	1669	561
% Writers	9.5	10.9*	14.3	16.4

TABLE 6.2   (Continued)

	Males		Females	
	Total Population	Accepted Population	Total Population	Accepted Population
EDITING (N)	2855	1230	1669	561
% Editors	12.8	14.6*	21.0	26.4***
DRAMATIC ARTS (N)	2855	1230	1669	561
% Dramatic arts involvement	7.5	8.6*	7.1	6.6
MUSIC (N)	2855	1230	1669	561
% Musicians	12.9	12.8	13.6	12.1
SCIENCE (N)	2855	1230	1669	561
% Science involvement	8.5	11.2***	7.1	8.6
ATHLETICS (N)	2855	1230	1669	561
% Athletes	15.8	12.2***	5.2	5.2
EMPLOYMENT (N)	2855	1230	1669	561
% Employed	18.9	18.2	4.7	4.5

either for parents' educational background or for financial-aid applicants, thus indicating that the decisions of the SAT and the actual committees have fairly similar effects as far as these two factors are concerned. On the other hand, there are marked differences as to the admission of non-whites, arising from the fact that the actual committee admits nonwhites while the SAT committee does not. Regarding other status characteristics upon which the two committees have consistent differential effects, applicants from the home state, applicants with alumni parents, and applicants from cities between 10,000 and 500,000 in population have a better chance at the hands of the actual committee than the SAT committee. The city size effect just mentioned undoubtedly is a by-product of the home-state effect, since the home state in question contains cities only in the aforementioned size bracket. There are almost no candidates acceptable on SAT grounds who have alumni connections or reside in the home state and are rejected by the actual committee, while there are sizable numbers of candidates with alumni affiliations or from the home state who are accepted by the actual committee but would be rejected by the SAT committee. On the whole, status differences between the actual class and the hypothetical SAT class stem generally from the actual committee's preferences for applicants from the home state, alumni children, and nonwhites.

Consider next the five personal characteristics of the applicants. Table 6.2 indicates that, as demanded by this particular admissions

TABLE 6.3   Characteristics of Applicants about Whom There Was Disagreement between the Admissions Decisions Made by the Actual Committee and the SAT Committee

	Males		Females	
	Actual Comm. Accepts, SAT Comm. Rejects	Actual Comm. Rejects, SAT Comm. Accepts	Actual Comm. Accepts, SAT Comm. Rejects	Actual Comm. Rejects, SAT Comm. Accepts
PARENT EDUCATION (N)	332	332	183	183
% Non-H.S. graduate	6.6	2.7*	3.3	3.8
% H.S. graduate	13.3	9.9	7.7	6.6
% Post-H.S., no degree	17.8	19.3	18.6	20.2
% College graduate	24.1	31.3	31.7	29.5
% Post-college	38.3	36.7	38.8	39.9
SCHOOL TYPE (N)	330	331	183	181
% Public	79.1	70.1*	77.6	79.0
% Parochial	3.0	6.3	1.1	3.3
% Private	17.9	23.6	21.3	17.7
TYPE OF HOME COMMUNITY (N)	332	332	183	183
% Metropolitan, > 1,000,000	11.1	20.5***	15.3	25.7**
% Suburban, < 1,000,000	6.6	19.9	14.2	21.3
% City, 500,000–1,000,000	1.8	2.7	3.3	1.6
% City, 100,000–500,000	19.9	10.5	15.8	5.5
% City, 10,000–100,000	37.3	33.1	36.6	28.4
% Town, < 10,000	17.8	10.5	10.9	13.1
% Farm or open country	5.4	2.7	3.8	4.4
COMMUNITY ECONOMIC RESOURCES (N)	332	332	183	183
% Agriculture	13.9	4.5***	4.4	4.9
% Heavy industry	6.3	6.0	13.7	9.3
% Light industry	16.6	5.7	11.5	9.3
% Residential	14.2	42.5	20.2	32.8
% Commerce	7.8	9.9	8.7	7.1
% Mining	0.9	0.0	0.5	0.0
% Diversified	40.4	31.3	41.0	36.6
PLACE OF RESIDENCE (N)	332	332	183	183
% Home state	39.8	0.6***	32.8	2.2***
% Regional, not home state	34.9	38.0	34.4	42.1
% Rest of U.S.	24.4	60.8	30.1	55.2
% Foreign	0.9	0.6	2.7	0.5

TABLE 6.3   (Continued)

	Males		Females	
	Actual Comm. Accepts, SAT Comm. Rejects	Actual Comm. Rejects, SAT Comm. Accepts	Actual Comm. Accepts, SAT Comm. Rejects	Actual Comm. Rejects, SAT Comm. Accepts
PARENT ALUMNI STATUS (N)	332	332	183	183
% Alumni	15.4	0.0***	19.7	1.6***
FINANCIAL AID (N)	332	332	183	183
% Aid applicants	48.5	34.9***	45.9	45.9
RACE (N)	332	332	183	183
% Nonwhite	5.4	0.0***	4.9	0.0**
SAT-V (N)	332	332	183	183
$\bar{X}$	574.59	636.58***	616.04	670.75***
SD	53.42	50.21	52.58	45.75
SAT-M (N)	332	332	183	183
$\bar{X}$	602.30	684.09***	591.39	667.19***
SD	56.49	44.37	55.00	44.93
TERMINAL DEGREE PLANS (N)	332	331	183	183
% BA, BS	12.3	11.2*	27.9	21.3
% MA, MS	21.4	24.8	46.4	47.0
% BD	0.0	0.3	0.0	0.0
% LLB	13.3	16.6	1.6	3.3
% MD	28.6	17.5	7.1	9.8
% PhD, EdD	24.4	29.6	16.9	18.6
PROPOSED MAJOR (N)	332	332	183	182
% Humanities	36.7	41.6*	57.9	41.2*
% Social sciences	9.9	11.4	10.9	15.9
% Bio. sciences	30.7	19.9	14.8	20.9
% Physical sciences	22.0	27.1	16.4	21.4
% Other	0.6	0.0	0.0	0.5
CAREER PLANS (N)	330	331	183	183
% Business	14.2	18.1*	6.6	4.9*
% Engineering	1.2	1.2	0.0	0.5
% Law	17.9	22.1	1.6	3.3
% Medicine	28.5	18.7	8.7	11.5
% Politics	3.6	4.2	3.8	2.7
% Science research	12.1	12.4	14.8	16.9
% Education	5.8	9.7	33.3	18.6
% Other	16.7	13.6	31.1	41.5
NMSC RECOGNITION (N)	332	332	183	183
% Recognized	15.7	35.5***	30.1	47.0***
CONVERTED CLASS RANK (N)	332	332	183	183
$\bar{X}$	64.95	58.16***	69.16	63.80***
SD	6.81	6.96	7.07	6.76

TABLE 6.3   (Continued)

	Males		Females	
	Actual Comm. Accepts, SAT Comm. Rejects	Actual Comm. Rejects, SAT Comm. Accepts	Actual Comm. Accepts, SAT Comm. Rejects	Actual Comm. Rejects, SAT Comm. Accepts
OVERALL NONACADEMIC ACCOMPLISHMENTS (N)	332	332	183	183
$\bar{X}$	9.16	8.02***	10.27	9.66
SD	3.74	3.49	3.48	3.67
LEADERSHIP (N)	332	332	183	183
% Leaders	19.6	14.8	7.7	4.9
ART (N)	332	332	183	183
% Artists	6.6	5.7	9.8	12.6
SOCIAL SERVICE (N)	332	332	183	183
% Social service involvement	22.0	17.2	23.0	15.8
WRITING (N)	332	332	183	183
% Writers	15.1	6.6***	14.8	11.5
EDITING (N)	332	332	183	183
% Editors	16.6	11.4	26.2	21.3
DRAMATIC ARTS (N)	332	332	183	183
% Dramatic arts involvement	9.0	5.7	9.3	7.1
MUSIC (N)	332	332	183	183
% Musicians	13.9	12.0	16.9	7.1**
SCIENCE (N)	332	332	183	183
% Science involvement	11.4	4.2***	9.3	6.6
ATHLETICS (N)	332	332	183	183
% Athletes	17.8	16.3	4.4	5.5
EMPLOYMENT (N)	332	332	183	183
% Employed	14.8	22.9**	3.3	6.6

model, the SAT scores for the accepted class are at the highest level that we shall witness compared to any other hypothetical class or to the actual class, and they are three quarters or more of a standard deviation above the means for the applicant population. Relatively speaking, the selection effects for other personal characteristics are modest. One can detect, however, consistent preferences for students with long-range educational goals over those seeking a bachelor's degree only; and for students with plans for a career in science. One also can detect consistent avoidance of students proposing to major in the humanities and of students interested in business administration. When the actual committee disagrees with the SAT committee, we find from Table 6.3 that the students favored by the actual committee have drastically lower mean SAT scores. Thus, despite the considerable overall agreement between SAT and actual committee selections, the latter's preference for high SAT scorers is sometimes countered by other preferences—as we saw, for example, in the results concerning status characteristics. Regarding terminal degree plans, proposed major, and career plans, nothing that is directionally consistent across the sexes differentiates the choices of the SAT committee from those of the actual committee.

We come now to accomplishment characteristics. As far as academic accomplishments are concerned, the SAT committee favors applicants with NMSC recognition and with high grades (Table 6.2), as was the case with the actual committee. Neither preference, of course, is particularly surprising. We have already noted how NMSC recognition reflects performance on intelligence-related tests and how academic achievement in high school is related to tested intelligence level. What about the candidates where the SAT and the actual committee are in disagreement? From Table 6.3 it may be seen that, for those cases where the two committees took opposing actions, the actual committee admits a significantly smaller proportion of NMSC-recognized applicants just as it admits a group with lower mean SAT scores. We also find from that table, however, that the candidates admitted by the actual but rejected by the SAT committee have much higher high school grade ranks than the candidates rejected by the actual but admitted by the SAT committee. In its propensity for choosing some candidates who have high ranks in class but relatively low SAT scores, the actual committee is demonstrating that it attaches considerable importance to achievement in high school over and above the degree to which such achievement is linked to SAT scores.

Turning to the nonacademic accomplishments of the candidates, a rather striking picture emerges. Table 6.2 indicates that, with the single exception of a preference for those with attainments as editors, there are no consistent preferences exhibited by the SAT committee regarding overall nonacademic accomplishments of the candidates or regarding the particular lines of endeavor that were considered singly— leadership, art, social service involvement, writing, editing, dramatic arts, music, science, athletics, and employment. Our evidence indicates therefore that a committee basing its decisions on the SAT score does not place any particular value on attainments outside of the academic arena. In other words, we find little if any linkage between level of SAT scores and level of nonacademic accomplishments. This outcome replicates with samples covering a broader range of SAT scores the results reported by Wallach and Wing (1969) in their earlier research. From Table 6.3 we note further that the actual committee is in essential agreement with the SAT committee in that there are no differential preference effects between the two yielding significant contrasts for both sexes in the case of any of the various measures of nonacademic attainments.

What, in summary, may we say about the characteristics of a class admitted by a committee basing its decisions on SAT scores only? Outside of having maximally high SAT scores, the class will be strong in its secondary school academic achievement. On the other hand, it will dis-proportionately under-represent culturally disadvantaged students—those who are nonwhite and those whose parents are less educated—and it will not contain any particular emphasis on talented nonacademic accomplishments. How, in turn, does the actual committee compare with the SAT committee? They are much alike in that they accept about seven tenths of the same male students and about two thirds of the same female students. Where the two committees disagree, it is because the actual committee is willing to accept lower SAT scores from students with sufficiently strong high school grades and from those with certain status characteristics (if they come from the home state, if they have alumni affiliations, and if they are nonwhite). Talented accomplishments outside the academic domain seem to play no systematic role in this regard.

The High School Rank Committee

Our second hypothetical admissions committee for selecting students on the basis of academic skills looks only at high school grade achievement. Like the SAT committee, the high school rank committee mirrors—imperfectly yet undeniably—a portion of the real world of admissions. In Chapter 2 we noted that many state-supported insti-tutions, faced with the need to distribute among the colleges and uni-versities of their own state systems the bulk of the high school graduates from their state, define their entrance requirements chiefly in terms of rank in high school class. These terms do not involve measures external to the state network of secondary schools such as scores on nationally administered tests. What often happens is that the "queen" institution of the state-supported system will accept only those students from the highest percentile ranks of the graduating high school classes. Virtually all of these students will be accepted; those with lower academic ratings are relegated to one of the satellite institutions. We also observed in the previous chapter that the actual admissions process at a typical high-selectivity private institution places considerable weight on the candidate's rank in high school class, and we noted earlier in this chapter the apparent importance of high school rank in accounting for instances where the actual committee accepts candidates whom the SAT committee rejects. We turn now to a direct study of the hypothetical class produced by an admissions committee that utilizes only the candidate's high school grade achievement in deciding whether to accept or reject. The applicants were ordered from highest to lowest, within sex, in terms of the single criterion of their converted high school class rank. They were accepted in descending order until the necessary quotas of males and females had been obtained. All the others were rejected.

Table 6.4 shows for the high school rank committee what Table 6.1 displayed for the SAT committee: it examines the degree of correspondence between the decisions made by the high school rank committee and by the actual committee. Once again frequencies of agreement and

TABLE 6.4   Extent of Decisional Agreement between the Actual Committee and the High School Rank Committee

	High School Rank Committee Admissions Decisions					
	Males			Females		
Actual Committee Admissions Decisions	Accept	Reject	Total Observed	Accept	Reject	Total Observed
Accept { Observed	836	352	1188	332	209	541
Accept { Expected	522	666		186	355	
Reject { Observed	352	1165	1517	209	823	1032
Reject { Expected	666	851		355	677	
Total observed			2705			1573

Predictive Accuracy	Males	Females
Error reduction index	47.1	41.1
% Decisions in agreement	74.0	73.4
% Acceptances in agreement	70.4	61.4

disagreement are presented and compared with what would be expected on a chance basis. It is obvious that the rank committee agrees with the actual committee far more than, and disagrees with it far less than, would be expected by chance alone. The error-reduction index values of 47.1 percent for the male population and 41.1 percent for the female population indicate that the chance rate of error is substantially reduced by applying the decision rule of the rank committee. Recalling that the respective values for the SAT committee were 50.2 percent and 48.5 percent, however, we can see that deciding by SAT scores alone results in greater reduction of error than deciding by high school rank alone. Comparing the two hypothetical committees in terms of the degree of overlap between each and the actual committee on acceptances in particular, we find that for the rank committee there is agreement with actuality on 70.4 percent of the male and 61.4 percent of the female acceptances. We recall that for the SAT committee there was agreement with the actual committee on 72.1 percent of the male and 66.2 percent of the female acceptances. While the SAT committee thus does a somewhat better job of predicting the actual class than the rank committee, it is clear nevertheless that a substantial majority of the applicants who gain admission by the actual committee would also be admitted by the rank committee.

How does a class assembled by the rank committee appear and in what respects does it differ from the actual class? To answer these questions we turn to Tables 6.5 and 6.6. Again we shall begin with status characteristics, then go on to personal characteristics, and conclude with accomplishment characteristics. We note from Table 6.5 that seven of the eight status characteristics under investigation yield statistically significant effects of consistent kinds for both sexes. The high school rank committee admits a class containing disproportionately more students whose parents did not go to college and disproportionately fewer students whose parents are college graduates, relative to the data for the applicant population as a whole. So also, this hypothetical class favors students from public high schools over those from private high schools; students from smaller cities and towns over those from large metropolitan and suburban areas; students who do not come from primarily residential areas; students from the home state and region; students who apply for financial aid; and students who are nonwhite. Compared with the total applicant pool, then, a rank-admitted class can be broadly described as biased toward the lower end of the socioeconomic spectrum (including greater representation of nonwhite applicants) and toward the geographical vicinity of the college. This kind of socioeconomic effect might be expected if students from lower socioeconomic backgrounds tend not to apply unless they have done relatively well in secondary school, while students from more affluent backgrounds apply despite relatively lower grade records.

Regarding the status characteristics of those candidates on whom the rank committee and the actual committee disagree, Table 6.6 indicates

TABLE 6.5   Characteristics of Total Applicant Population and of Population Accepted by the High School Rank Committee

	Males		Females	
	Total Population	Accepted Population	Total Population	Accepted Population
PARENT EDUCATION (N)	2755	1189	1592	544
% Non-H.S. graduate	4.5	6.1***	4.7	6.8***
% H.S. graduate	10.8	12.4	8.5	11.4
% Post-H.S., no degree	20.5	21.6	19.7	20.4
% College graduate	28.7	26.6	26.6	24.8
% Post-college	35.5	33.3	40.5	36.6
SCHOOL TYPE (N)	2750	1187	1586	540
% Public	72.9	86.6***	79.2	92.8***
% Parochial	4.4	3.3	2.4	0.9
% Private	22.6	10.1	18.4	6.3
TYPE OF HOME COMMUNITY (N)	2753	1188	1588	544
% Metropolitan, > 1,000,000	15.8	13.8***	17.9	12.5***
% Suburban, < 1,000,000	17.5	14.5	18.0	15.1
% City, 500,000–1,000,000	2.2	2.1	2.6	2.6
% City, 100,000–500,000	14.1	15.7	12.5	13.2
% City, 10,000–100,000	32.3	34.3	32.2	35.8
% Town, < 10,000	14.0	15.2	11.9	14.9
% Farm or open country	4.2	4.5	4.8	5.9
COMMUNITY ECONOMIC RESOURCES (N)	2751	1186	1589	543
% Agriculture	8.0	9.0***	6.2	7.6*
% Heavy industry	7.7	7.7	8.6	9.6
% Light industry	10.1	11.0	11.1	13.1
% Residential	30.9	25.2	29.5	24.9
% Commerce	7.4	7.5	6.4	5.7
% Mining	0.5	0.4	0.6	1.1
% Diversified	35.5	39.1	37.6	38.1
PLACE OF RESIDENCE (N)	2754	1189	1591	544
% Home state	10.3	14.6***	12.9	19.7***
% Regional, not home state	37.6	42.5	39.0	42.8
% Rest of U.S.	50.8	42.2	46.0	36.4
% Foreign	1.3	0.8	2.1	1.1
PARENT ALUMNI STATUS (N)	2754	1188	1592	544
% Alumni	4.8	4.7	7.0	7.0
FINANCIAL AID (N)	2755	1189	1592	544
% Aid applicants	39.7	56.3***	41.8	58.1***
RACE (N)	2755	1189	1592	544
% Nonwhite	0.9	1.7***	2.1	4.2***
SAT-V (N)	2705	1180	1573	535
$\bar{X}$	594.20	619.97***	616.92	641.93***
SD	82.45	77.55	80.90	75.97

TABLE 6.5   (Continued)

	Males		Females	
	Total Population	Accepted Population	Total Population	Accepted Population
SAT-M (N)	2706	1180	1573	535
$\bar{X}$	636.40	662.39***	609.69	632.74***
SD	79.51	74.63	79.43	78.65
TERMINAL DEGREE PLANS (N)	2750	1188	1591	544
% BA, BS	13.0	7.7***	30.7	22.4***
% MA, MS	23.7	20.2	44.3	49.3
% BD	0.4	0.3	0.1	0.0
% LLB	14.2	12.4	2.3	2.4
% MD	22.9	25.2	9.1	9.2
% PhD, EdD	25.8	34.2	13.6	16.7
PROPOSED MAJOR (N)	2754	1188	1591	543
% Humanities	37.2	30.1***	53.5	49.7
% Social sciences	9.7	11.7	12.0	11.8
% Bio. sciences	25.8	28.6	17.2	17.5
% Physical sciences	27.0	29.4	17.1	20.8
% Other	0.3	0.3	0.2	0.2
CAREER PLANS (N)	2746	1185	1591	543
% Business	16.5	11.7***	5.8	5.3*
% Engineering	1.3	1.3	0.3	0.2
% Law	19.1	16.4	2.8	3.5
% Medicine	23.9	26.6	10.4	9.9
% Politics	3.5	3.5	2.4	1.5
% Science research	14.1	18.7	13.2	16.9
% Education	6.7	7.2	26.1	26.2
% Other	14.9	14.7	39.1	36.5
NMSC RECOGNITION (N)	2755	1189	1592	544
% Recognized	26.6	39.2***	29.6	43.6***
CONVERTED CLASS RANK (N)	2755	1189	1592	544
$\bar{X}$	61.75	68.91***	65.50	73.28***
SD	8.07	4.12	7.50	3.20
OVERALL NONACADEMIC ACCOMPLISHMENTS (N)	2755	1189	1592	544
$\bar{X}$	8.31	9.08***	9.82	10.25***
SD	3.78	3.67	3.57	3.51
LEADERSHIP (N)	2755	1189	1592	544
% Leaders	17.0	21.3***	8.0	8.8
ART (N)	2755	1189	1592	544
% Artists	5.1	4.5	11.9	11.0
SOCIAL SERVICE (N)	2755	1189	1592	544
% Social service involvement	20.1	21.1	19.8	23.2*
WRITING (N)	2755	1189	1592	544
% Writers	9.5	12.4***	14.6	18.0**

TABLE 6.5   (Continued)

	Males		Females	
	Total Population	Accepted Population	Total Population	Accepted Population
EDITING (N)	2755	1189	1592	544
% Editors	12.7	16.8***	20.9	25.2**
DRAMATIC ARTS (N)	2755	1189	1592	544
% Dramatic arts involvement	7.5	10.1***	6.9	8.6*
MUSIC (N)	2755	1189	1592	544
% Musicians	13.0	13.5	13.4	16.9**
SCIENCE (N)	2755	1189	1592	544
% Science involvement	8.4	13.7***	7.3	12.7***
ATHLETICS (N)	2755	1189	1592	544
% Athletes	16.4	13.0***	5.2	5.0
EMPLOYMENT (N)	2755	1189	1592	544
% Employed	18.7	16.1**	4.7	3.5

that the students favored by the actual committee are more likely to come from family backgrounds with higher educational status, from private rather than public high schools, from more populous home communities, from the home state and from alumni backgrounds. Also they are less likely to request financial aid. The effects resulting from educational level of parents, type of high school attended, population of home community, and financial aid suggest that the high school rank committee tends toward admitting a larger proportion of students from what might be called culturally disadvantaged backgrounds while the actual committee tends to favor a more advantaged group. Perhaps the actual committee is hesitant to rely upon superior high school performance when that performance takes place in school and community contexts not considered to be of "the best." The effects of home state residence and alumni background, in turn, indicate once again the actual committee's preference for home team candidates—a preference that was displayed as well when we compared the choices of the actual committee with those of the SAT committee.

In contrast to the aforementioned differences on status characteristics it should be noted that the attitude of the actual committee toward nonwhites is more similar to that of the high school rank committee than to that of the SAT committee. The tendency of the rank committee to favor nonwhite applicants is preserved in the actions of the actual committee for males, although not for females.

Consider next the personal characteristics of the candidates chosen

TABLE 6.6   Characteristics of Applicants about Whom There Was Disagreement between the Admissions Decisions Made by the Actual Committee and the High School Rank Committee

	Males		Females	
	Actual Comm. Accepts, High School Rank Comm. Rejects	Actual Comm. Rejects, High School Rank Comm. Accepts	Actual Comm. Accepts, High School Rank Comm. Rejects	Actual Comm. Rejects, High School Rank Comm. Accepts
PARENT EDUCATION (N)	352	352	209	209
% Non-H.S. graduate	3.1	8.5***	2.4	10.5***
% H.S. graduate	9.1	15.3	3.3	13.9
% Post-H.S., no degree	14.5	22.7	14.8	22.5
% College graduate	29.8	27.0	34.9	16.3
% Post-college	43.5	26.4	44.5	36.8
SCHOOL TYPE (N)	351	352	208	206
% Public	53.8	82.7***	58.7	96.1***
% Parochial	2.8	5.7	1.9	0.0
% Private	43.3	11.6	39.4	3.9
TYPE OF HOME COMMUNITY (N)	351	351	209	209
% Metropolitan, > 1,000,000	19.9	12.5**	21.5	10.0*
% Suburban, < 1,000,000	15.1	14.5	17.7	16.3
% City, 500,000– 1,000,000	2.0	3.4	3.3	2.9
% City, 100,000– 500,000	17.4	10.5	11.0	9.6
% City, 10,000– 100,000	27.6	37.3	31.1	35.4
% Town, < 10,000	14.2	16.5	10.5	18.7
% Farm or open country	3.7	5.1	4.8	7.2
COMMUNITY ECONOMIC RESOURCES (N)	351	352	209	208
% Agriculture	9.7	10.8	4.3	10.6*
% Heavy industry	4.8	7.4	7.2	7.7
% Light industry	9.7	10.5	10.0	14.9
% Residential	28.2	28.1	34.0	27.4
% Commerce	8.0	8.2	8.1	3.8
% Mining	0.0	0.0	1.0	1.9
% Diversified	39.6	34.9	35.4	33.7
PLACE OF RESIDENCE (N)	351	352	209	209
% Home state	20.8	4.5***	18.7	12.0**
% Regional, not home state	33.6	43.2	29.7	45.0
% Rest of U.S.	43.3	51.4	49.3	42.1
% Foreign	2.3	0.9	2.4	1.0

TABLE 6.6   (Continued)

	Males		Females	
	Actual Comm. Accepts, High School Rank Comm. Rejects	Actual Comm. Rejects, High School Rank Comm. Accepts	Actual Comm. Accepts, High School Rank Comm. Rejects	Actual Comm. Rejects, High School Rank Comm. Accepts
PARENT ALUMNI				
STATUS (N)	352	352	209	209
% Alumni	13.4	1.4***	14.8	2.4***
FINANCIAL AID (N)	352	352	209	209
% Aid applicants	34.7	46.9***	38.3	54.5***
RACE (N)	352	352	209	209
% Nonwhite	0.9	1.1	0.5	6.2**
SAT-V (N)	352	352	209	209
$\bar{X}$	633.84	557.22***	667.87	593.48***
SD	67.31	63.28	62.41	72.77
SAT-M (N)	352	352	209	209
$\bar{X}$	659.61	614.14***	646.29	587.56***
SD	68.28	66.75	68.04	76.42
TERMINAL DEGREE				
PLANS (N)	352	351	209	209
% BA, BS	13.1	9.7	31.6	24.4
% MA, MS	24.1	22.2	44.0	47.8
% BD	0.0	0.9	0.0	0.0
% LLB	17.3	13.4	2.4	3.3
% MD	22.2	27.9	7.7	8.6
% PhD, EdD	23.3	25.9	14.4	15.8
PROPOSED MAJOR (N)	352	352	209	208
% Humanities	42.6	30.1**	62.7	50.0
% Social sciences	11.1	10.5	11.5	11.5
% Bio. sciences	23.9	29.8	12.0	20.2
% Physical sciences	21.9	29.5	13.9	17.8
% Other	0.6	0.0	0.0	0.5
CAREER PLANS (N)	352	351	209	209
% Business	15.6	16.0	4.8	7.7
% Engineering	1.4	0.9	0.0	0.5
% Law	23.6	18.2	1.9	4.8
% Medicine	22.2	30.2	8.1	9.1
% Politics	3.7	2.8	4.8	2.4
% Science research	12.2	12.3	11.0	15.3
% Education	6.5	5.1	24.9	27.3
% Other	14.8	14.5	44.5	33.0
NMSC RECOGNITION (N)	352	352	209	209
% Recognized	38.6	9.4***	46.9	19.6***
CONVERTED CLASS				
RANK (N)	352	352	209	209
$\bar{X}$	58.71	67.05***	63.54	72.11***
SD	4.39	3.01	4.60	3.00

TABLE 6.6   (Continued)

	Males		Females	
	Actual Comm. Accepts, High School Rank Comm. Rejects	Actual Comm. Rejects, High School Rank Comm. Accepts	Actual Comm. Accepts, High School Rank Comm. Rejects	Actual Comm. Rejects, High School Rank Comm. Accepts
OVERALL NONACADEMIC ACCOMPLISHMENTS (N)	352	352	209	209
$\bar{X}$	8.58	8.39	10.11	10.16
SD	3.90	3.68	3.55	3.66
LEADERSHIP (N)	352	352	209	209
% Leaders	15.9	23.0*	10.5	10.0
ART (N)	352	352	209	209
% Artists	4.8	5.7	11.5	14.8
SOCIAL SERVICE (N)	352	352	209	209
% Social service involvement	21.6	21.6	18.2	23.9
WRITING (N)	352	352	209	209
% Writers	10.8	7.4	15.3	15.3
EDITING (N)	352	352	209	209
% Editors	13.4	16.2	28.7	21.5
DRAMATIC ARTS (N)	352	352	209	209
% Dramatic arts involvement	7.1	8.5	4.8	9.1
MUSIC (N)	352	352	209	209
% Musicians	12.5	11.4	12.4	16.3
SCIENCE (N)	352	352	209	209
% Science involvement	6.3	7.7	3.8	11.5**
ATHLETICS (N)	352	352	209	209
% Athletes	16.5	16.8	3.8	5.3
EMPLOYMENT (N)	352	352	209	209
% Employed	17.3	18.2	3.8	4.3

by the high school rank committee. Four of the five variables show statistically significant effects of congruent kinds for males and females, as shown in Table 6.5. Not surprisingly, the population accepted by the rank committee has higher SAT-V and SAT-M scores as well—a finding in accord with the generally high positive relationship between secondary school grade rank and SAT scores. Thus, if a committee shows preferences for students high on one of these measures, the students selected are apt also to be high on the other. However, from Table 6.6 it is evident that the actual committee places still greater weight on SAT scores than the degree of emphasis they receive by virtue of their linkage with secondary school grades: applicants accepted by the actual committee but rejected by the rank committee have SAT scores that are considerably higher than those of applicants rejected by the actual committee but accepted by the rank committee. Turning to other personal characteristics, we find in Table 6.5 that the candidates chosen by the rank committee are more likely to be planning work beyond the bachelor's degree level and less likely to be planning terminal degrees at the bachelor's level, and are more likely to be planning scientific careers. The actual committee does not differ particularly here from the rank committee as to effects, since Table 6.6 indicates no differences in these characteristics for applicants about whom the rank and actual committees made opposite decisons.

Characteristics reflecting academic accomplishment—National Merit Scholarship Corporation recognition and high school grades—show substantial differences favoring the class accepted by the rank committee (Table 6.5). The rank committee favors applicants recognized by NMSC, of course, since grade rank is associated with intelligence test scores which, in turn, are associated with NMSC recognition. But Table 6.6 shows that the actual committee admits an even higher proportion of NMSC-recognized candidates than does the rank committee, as indicated by considering those candidates on whom the two committees disagree. This finding dovetails with the discovery that the actual committee also places greater emphasis upon SAT scores than does the rank committee, given the similarity between the SAT and the tests performance on which is reflected in NMSC recognition. Turning to high school grades, these must inevitably receive substantial emphasis in the groups selected for admission by the rank committee (Table 6.5), since grade rank constituted the basis of its selection policy. But note from Table 6.6 that the degree of this emphasis is too great for the actual committee's taste. Where the two committees disagree, those accepted by the actual committee have substantially lower high school grades than those accepted by the rank committee.

What about the effects of the rank committee on the nonacademic forms of accomplishment displayed by the class it selects? Table 6.5 indicates modest but consistent enhancements for overall nonacademic accomplishments and for specific attainments in the areas of writing, editing, drama, and science. No consistent effects emerge for the remaining six areas. Table 6.6 indicates that the actual committee does not differ particularly from the rank committee in regard to policy affecting the nonacademic attainment characteristics of the students selected. The rank committee thus seems to give a small but consistent preference to certain nonacademic accomplishments of applicants. The actual committee tends to act in a similar way.

Let us summarize now the major characteristics of a class selected by a high school rank committee and how these characteristics compare with those of a class selected by an actual admissions committee. The SAT scores of the rank committee's class are increased, relative to the applicant pool, but they are not increased to a level high enough to suit the actual committee. Secondary school grade quality, on the other hand—which is of course as high as it can be in the class selected by the rank committee—is higher than in the actual committee's class. Thus the actual committee places more emphasis on SAT scores and less emphasis on grades than the rank committee. The rank committee tends to emphasize applicants from what might be termed lower socioeconomic or culturally disadvantaged backgrounds—an emphasis that is not shared by the actual committee except in cases where the applicant is nonwhite and male. The actual committee's class tends to resemble the SAT committee's class more closely than the rank committee's class. Of course, the actual committee differs from both the rank committee and the SAT committee in the matter of home team preferences, favoring applicants from the home state of the university and from alumni-connected families. Finally, as to accomplishments in nonacademic areas, the rank committee seems to admit a group slightly more talented in these respects than those it rejects, and the actual committee tends to agree with these leanings.

Agreement and Disagreement between SAT and High School Rank Committees

Having explored the effects of SAT-based and high school rank-based selection policies upon the characteristics of hypothetically chosen classes, let us examine the similarities and differences between these two approaches. Direct comparison should make more explicit certain outcomes we observed when comparing each committee's hypothetical class with the class chosen by the actual committee.

Consider first in Table 6.7 the extent to which the SAT and the rank committees agree in the classes they select. While the level of agreement is above chance expectancies, the values of the error-reduction indexes (26.6 percent for males and 22.0 percent for females) are way below what they were when comparing either hypothetical committee with the actual committee. In the same way, the proportions of all decisions that were in agreement and the proportions of acceptances that were in agree-

TABLE 6.7   Extent of Decisional Agreement between the
SAT Committee and the High School Rank Committee

SAT Committee Admissions Decisions		High School Rank Committee Admissions Decisions					
		Males			Females		
		Accept	Reject	Total Observed	Accept	Reject	Total Observed
Accept { Observed		699	489	1188	264	277	541
Expected		522	666		186	355	
Reject { Observed		489	1028	1517	277	755	1032
Expected		666	851		355	677	
Total observed				2705			1573

Predictive Accuracy	Males	Females
Error-reduction index	26.6	22.0
% Decisions in agreement	63.8	64.8
% Acceptances in agreement	58.8	48.8

ment are considerably lower between the SAT and rank committees than they were between either hypothetical committee and the actual committee. This much disagreement suggests how different can be the effects of two selection policies even when both are choosing classes in terms of indicators of academic skills and when we know that the indicators are related to each other. Applicants may self-select themselves to some extent, applying if their SAT scores are relatively high even though their grades are not so high, or if their grades are relatively high even though their SAT scores are not so high. Then what are the differences between admitting a class in terms of SAT scores and admitting a class in terms of secondary school grades? We turn now to the cases where the SAT committee and the rank committee disagreed in their actions, in order to determine what student characteristics besides SAT scores and secondary school grade quality receive differential emphasis at the hands of the two committees.

Table 6.8 compares the applicants accepted by the SAT committee but rejected by the rank committee with the applicants rejected by the SAT committee but accepted by the rank committee. The comparison made here is essentially between a group of candidates high in SAT scores and low in class rank, and a group of candidates low in SAT scores and high in class rank. Because there was considerable disagreement between the admissions actions of the SAT and rank committees, the numbers in

TABLE 6.8   Characteristics of Applicants about Whom There Was Disagreement between the Admissions Decisions Made by the SAT Committee and the High School Rank Committee

	Males		Females	
	SAT Comm. Accepts, High School Rank Comm. Rejects	SAT Comm. Rejects, High School Rank Comm. Accepts	SAT Comm. Accepts, High School Rank Comm. Rejects	SAT Comm. Rejects, High School Rank Comm. Accepts
PARENT EDUCATION (N)	489	489	277	277
% Non-H.S. graduate	1.8	8.4***	3.2	9.0***
% H.S. graduate	8.0	14.7	5.4	14.1
% Post-H.S., no degree	16.8	21.7	17.0	21.7
% College graduate	32.5	25.6	32.9	20.2
% Post-college	40.9	29.7	41.5	35.0
SCHOOL TYPE (N)	488	488	276	276
% Public	58.2	85.0***	66.3	93.5***
% Parochial	3.5	3.3	3.3	0.4
% Private	38.3	11.7	30.4	6.2
TYPE OF HOME COMMUNITY (N)	488	488	277	277
% Metropolitan, > 1,000,000	22.5	10.9***	25.3	9.7***
% Suburban, < 1,000,000	20.9	11.5	18.4	12.6
% City, 500,000– 1,000,000	2.5	2.9	2.5	3.2
% City, 100,000– 500,000	13.3	14.8	7.9	13.7
% City, 10,000– 100,000	27.5	37.3	30.3	39.0
% Town, < 10,000	10.7	17.2	10.1	14.8
% Farm or open country	2.7	5.5	5.4	6.9
COMMUNITY ECONOMIC RESOURCES (N)	488	489	277	276
% Agriculture	5.1	12.3***	4.7	9.1**
% Heavy industry	5.1	7.2	6.9	10.1
% Light industry	7.6	15.5	9.0	14.1
% Residential	39.5	20.2	34.3	21.0
% Commerce	9.2	8.0	6.9	4.7
% Mining	0.0	0.6	0.7	1.8
% Diversified	33.4	36.2	37.5	39.1
PLACE OF RESIDENCE (N)	488	489	277	277
% Home state	5.5	20.4***	6.5	21.7***
% Regional, not home state	36.1	40.9	37.9	44.4
% Rest of U.S.	56.8	37.8	54.2	32.1
% Foreign	1.6	0.8	1.4	1.8

TABLE 6.8   (Continued)

	Males		Females	
	SAT Comm. Accepts, High School Rank Comm. Rejects	SAT Comm. Rejects, High School Rank Comm. Accepts	SAT Comm. Accepts, High School Rank Comm. Rejects	SAT Comm. Rejects, High School Rank Comm. Accepts
PARENT ALUMNI				
STATUS (N)	489	489	277	277
% Alumni	3.7	5.5	4.7	7.2
FINANCIAL AID (N)	489	489	277	277
% Aid applicants	33.5	51.5***	42.2	54.5**
RACE (N)	489	489	277	277
% Nonwhite	0.0	3.9***	0.0	7.6***
SAT-V (N)	489	489	277	277
$\bar{X}$	652.69	555.45***	685.26	592.99***
SD	51.08	57.20	45.24	64.71
SAT-M (N)	489	489	277	277
$\bar{X}$	687.14	598.88***	672.90	578.52***
SD	45.92	56.32	46.74	64.66
TERMINAL DEGREE				
PLANS (N)	488	488	277	277
% BA, BS	12.3	10.7***	27.8	26.7
% MA, MS	25.4	21.7	44.0	46.6
% BD	0.0	0.4	0.0	0.0
% LLB	17.2	12.1	2.9	2.5
% MD	18.4	30.1	8.7	7.6
% PhD, EdD	26.6	25.0	16.6	16.6
PROPOSED MAJOR (N)	489	489	277	277
% Humanities	42.1	29.9***	50.2	51.6
% Social sciences	12.1	10.6	15.2	11.9
% Bio. sciences	20.9	32.5	15.2	17.3
% Physical sciences	24.7	26.8	19.1	18.8
% Other	0.2	0.2	0.4	0.4
CAREER PLANS (N)	488	486	277	277
% Business	16.6	14.2***	4.3	7.6**
% Engineering	1.4	1.0	0.4	0.4
% Law	22.7	16.0	2.5	3.6
% Medicine	10.1	31.5	9.4	8.3
% Politics	3.9	2.9	3.2	2.2
% Science research	13.7	13.6	14.1	15.9
% Education	9.2	5.6	18.8	30.3
% Other	13.3	15.2	47.3	31.8
NMSC RECOGNITION (N)	489	489	277	277
% Recognized	45.0	10.4***	54.9	23.1***
CONVERTED CLASS				
RANK (N)	489	489	277	277
$\bar{X}$	47.30	67.92***	62.75	72.75***
SD	5.29	3.58	5.00	3.27

TABLE 6.8   (Continued)

	Males		Females	
	SAT Comm. Accepts, High School Rank Comm. Rejects	SAT Comm. Rejects, High School Rank Comm. Accepts	SAT Comm. Accepts, High School Rank Comm. Rejects	SAT Comm. Rejects, High School Rank Comm. Accepts
OVERALL NONACADEMIC ACCOMPLISHMENTS (N)	489	489	277	277
$\bar{X}$	8.23	8.86**	9.88	10.32
SD	3.66	3.68	3.56	3.50
LEADERSHIP (N)	489	489	277	277
% Leaders	13.7	22.1***	8.3	9.7
ART (N)	489	489	277	277
% Artists	4.3	5.5	11.9	12.6
SOCIAL SERVICE (N)	489	489	277	277
% Social service involvement	18.0	21.3	17.0	26.0**
WRITING (N)	489	489	277	277
% Writers	8.2	11.5	14.8	17.0
EDITING (N)	489	489	277	277
% Editors	11.7	17.2*	27.1	24.9
DRAMATIC ARTS (N)	489	489	277	277
% Dramatic arts involvement	6.5	9.8	5.1	9.7*
MUSIC (N)	489	489	277	277
% Musicians	12.1	12.5	9.4	18.8**
SCIENCE (N)	489	489	277	277
% Science involvement	4.7	10.6***	4.0	11.6***
ATHLETICS (N)	489	489	277	277
% Athletes	14.5	15.7	4.3	4.7
EMPLOYMENT (N)	489	489	277	277
% Employed	21.3	16.4*	5.1	3.2

the groups for this analysis are substantially larger than they were for the comparable analyses concerning cases of disagreement between each hypothetical committee and the actual committee. Besides the necessary differences between these two groups in SAT scores and secondary school rank, we find from Table 6.8 that the groups are strikingly different in ways consistent for both sexes regarding all of the status attributes but one—alumni affiliation. Personal characteristics other than SAT scores show no clear differences that are directionally congruent for both sexes. As far as academic forms of achievement are concerned, NMSC recognition characterizes much higher proportions for each sex of the high SAT-low class rank group than of the low SAT-high class rank group—a finding consistent once again with the way in which NMSC recognition is reflective of performance on intelligence-related tests. Regarding non-academic forms of accomplishments, the groups show no consistent differences with the single exception of science involvement, which is greater for the low SAT-high class rank group. But let us return to the pervasive status differences between the groups. We see that it is only in this area that the two hypothetical committees exert major differential impact, apart from the SAT and grade rank contrasts necessitated by their definition.

The status effects reported in Table 6.8 fall into a clear pattern. The candidates who are accepted by the rank committee but rejected by the SAT committee, whether male or female, include higher proportions of applicants who are from families where the parents do not have a college degree; who went to public school, who come from communities with populations under 500,000 where the major economic resources are agricultural or industrial; who are from the state or the region where the university is located; who request financial aid; and who are nonwhite. On the other hand, the candidates who are accepted by the SAT committee but rejected by the rank committee, whether male or female, include higher proportions of applicants who are from families where the parents are college graduates or even have post-college education; who went to private high school; who are from big cities or residential suburbs; who are from outside the region; who do not request financial aid; and who are white. It is evident from these status contrasts that the SAT committee in general favors those who are more advantaged culturally or socioeconomically, while the rank committee is more responsive to those from disadvantaged backgrounds. This was the conclusion suggested by our earlier analyses, and it receives strong direct confirmation in the present comparison.

The SAT plus High School Rank Committee

If, as we suggested when introducing our consideration of the SAT and the high school rank committees, each committee mirrors to a degree the real world of college admissions, then the hypothetical committee that we now present may possess even stronger claims in this regard. Many institutions sufficiently in demand to utilize selective admissions policies combine scores on intelligence tests with measures of past academic performance to provide, as discussed in Chapter 1, a single index of applicant merit which then receives attention in the admissions process. Consistent with the expectation that both intelligence test scores and secondary school grades play substantial roles in admissions decisions, we have found in the present chapter that both the SAT committee and the high school rank committee predict the decisions made by the actual committee more accurately than they predict the decisions made by each other. A combination of the two into a hypothetical committee basing its decisions on SAT scores and secondary school grade achievement considered jointly should, by this reasoning, predict the composition of the actual class even more accurately than we have been able to do thus far.

In devising a hypothetical committee that would take into account both the SAT scores and the high school grade ranks of the candidates, we had to decide what relative weights to assign to the SAT, with its separate verbal and mathematical scores, and to secondary school grade rank, in order to achieve a unified measure for ranking the candidates in a single order. We tried two different combinations—one which gave equal weights to SAT-V scores, SAT-M scores, and high school rank, thus giving SAT scores twice the weight of high school grades, and one which gave SAT-V scores one-sixth weight, SAT-M scores one-sixth weight, and grades two-thirds weight, thus giving grades twice the weight of SAT scores. Grades and the SAT each receive substantial emphasis, of course, with either method of combination. Since both methods yielded highly comparable results in predicting actual committee decisions, we shall present only the outcomes for the former—equal weights to SAT-V scores, SAT-M scores, and high school rank. It is in fact the same weighting arrangement that we used in the earlier research described in Chapter 3, and it takes its specific rationale from our having found that use of SAT scores (SAT-V plus SAT-M) alone predicts actual committee decisions more accurately than does use of high school grade rank alone. Our SAT plus high school rank committee, then, assigns each applicant a rank order location for relative acceptability simply by summing standard scored and hence equally weighted transformations of his SAT-V score, SAT-M score, and rank in high school class.

Table 6.9 tells us how well the decisions of the SAT plus high school rank committee agree with those made by the actual committee. The level of agreement obtained is higher than that found for either the SAT committee or the rank committee, and it is clear that in absolute terms the extent of agreement is very great indeed. For the men, the error reduction index has climbed to 59.5 percent, 80 percent of all decisions are in agreement, and 77.3 percent of the acceptance decisions are in agreement. The picture for the women is similar: 56.3 percent is the

TABLE 6.9 Extent of Decisional Agreement between the Actual Committee and the SAT plus High School Rank Committee

| | SAT plus High School Rank Committee Admissions Decisions | | | | | |
| | Males | | | Females | | |
Actual Committee Admissions Decisions	Accept	Reject	Total Observed	Accept	Reject	Total Observed
Accept {Observed	918	270	1188	386	155	541
Accept {Expected	522	666		186	355	
Reject {Observed	270	1247	1517	155	877	1032
Reject {Expected	666	851		355	677	
Total observed			2705			1573

Predictive Accuracy	Males	Females
Error-reduction index	59.5	56.3
% Decisions in agreement	80.0	80.3
% Acceptances in agreement	77.3	71.3

value of the error-reduction index, 80.3 percent of all decisions are in agreement, and 71.3 percent of the decisions about acceptances are in agreement. These findings replicate, therefore, the research outcomes described in Chapter 3. Once again we find that predicting actual committee decisions from information about SAT scores and class ranks of the candidates makes for greater accuracy than using either type of information alone. Once again, too, we come to the conclusion that a decision model based only on SAT scores and rank in high school class, crude and simple as it is, predicts with an amazing degree of accuracy the decisions that will be made by an actual admissions committee. Well over half of the error that would occur by chance is eliminated if one merely uses this quite elementary decision rule.

Given this considerable degree of correspondence between the decisions of the actual committee and those of the SAT plus high school rank committee, how does the class which the SAT plus rank committee admits compare to those who apply? Also, can one locate the specific remaining sources of discrepancy between the classes chosen by the SAT plus rank committee and by the actual committee? In particular, do these remaining discrepancies arise because the actual committee takes into account, through its decision-making, talented attainments in nonacademic pursuits? To answer these questions we turn to Tables 6.10 and 6.11. Table 6.10 describes the characteristics of the population accepted by the SAT plus rank committee against the background of the characteristics of the total applicant pool, and Table 6.11 compares the characteristics of the students concerning whom the actual committee and the SAT plus rank committee made opposite decisions.

What status characteristics end up receiving differential emphasis compared to their base-rates in the applicant pool when the SAT plus rank committee decides on admissions? We find from Table 6.10 that only three of the eight status characteristics are affected in a consistent way for both sexes by this hypothetical committee—it favors those with public school rather than private school backgrounds, it favors those applying for financial aid, and it favors whites over nonwhites. What does the actual committee do, in turn, that is different from the SAT plus rank committee regarding effects on status characteristics? From Table 6.11 we find that those students admitted by the actual but rejected by the SAT plus rank committee, compared to those rejected by the actual but admitted by the SAT plus rank committee, include for both sexes more applicants from private schools, from medium-sized cities and from the home state; more who have alumni affiliations, and more who are nonwhite. Most notably discrepancies between the actual committee's choices and those of the SAT plus rank committee with respect to status characteristics reflect the actual committee's favoring of applicants from private schools, applicants from the home state, applicants with alumni affiliations, and applicants who are nonwhite.

Next let us consider effects on personal characteristics. Table 6.10 indicates that the class accepted by the SAT plus rank committee possesses considerably heightened SAT-V and SAT-M scores relative to the applicant pool—hardly a surprising outcome since SAT scores comprised part of the explicit selection rule of this hypothetical committee. We note from Table 6.11, however, that the actual committee diminishes this emphasis somewhat although it is an emphasis which the actual committee shares in large part. What Table 6.11 indicates is that when the actual committee accepts students rejected by the SAT plus rank committee, the decisions of the actual committee have the effect of lowering the SAT-score level of the class. Other factors are outweighing SAT scores as determinants of the actual committee's actions in these cases, and we already know that home-state residence, alumni affiliation, and nonwhite racial status are among the preferred factors in question. As to the remaining personal characteristics, the SAT plus rank committee tends to favor students planning to obtain graduate school doctorates and not those planning to terminate their education with a bachelor's degree; and tends to favor students planning careers in science

TABLE 6.10   Characteristics of Total Applicant Population
and of Population Accepted by the SAT plus High School
Rank Committee

	Males		Females	
	Total Population	Accepted Population	Total Population	Accepted Population
PARENT EDUCATION (N)	2705	1188	1573	541
% Non-H.S. graduate	4.4	3.8	4.6	3.9
% H.S. graduate	10.7	10.7	8.5	8.3
% Post-H.S., no degree	20.3	20.6	19.6	19.0
% College graduate	28.8	27.8	26.7	29.9
% Post-college	35.8	37.1	40.6	38.8
SCHOOL TYPE (N)	2700	1185	1567	537
% Public	72.9	82.0***	79.1	85.7***
% Parochial	4.3	2.8	2.4	1.9
% Private	22.8	15.2	18.5	12.5
TYPE OF HOME COMMUNITY (N)	2703	1187	1569	541
% Metropolitan, > 1,000,000	15.6	16.6	18.0	17.4
% Suburban, < 1,000,000	17.6	16.9	17.9	17.0
% City, 500,000–1,000,000	2.2	1.9	2.7	2.2
% City, 100,000–500,000	14.1	16.1	12.4	11.1
% City, 10,000–100,000	32.3	31.5	32.4	32.9
% Town, < 10,000	13.9	13.5	11.9	14.0
% Farm or open country	4.3	3.5	4.7	5.4
COMMUNITY ECONOMIC RESOURCES (N)	2701	1184	1570	541
% Agriculture	7.9	6.8**	6.2	6.3
% Heavy industry	7.6	6.9	8.6	7.6
% Light industry	10.0	8.5	11.1	11.1
% Residential	30.9	30.6	29.5	30.9
% Commerce	7.6	7.4	6.4	6.5
% Mining	0.4	0.3	0.6	0.4
% Diversified	35.6	39.4	37.6	37.3
PLACE OF RESIDENCE (N)	2704	1187	1572	541
% Home state	10.5	10.0**	13.0	13.9
% Regional, not home state	37.8	41.9	38.7	40.9
% Rest of U.S.	50.4	47.2	46.1	44.2
% Foreign	1.3	0.9	2.1	1.1
PARENT ALUMNI STATUS (N)	2704	1187	1573	541
% Alumni	4.9	4.5	7.1	5.7
FINANCIAL AID (N)	2705	1188	1573	541
% Aid applicants	39.6	53.0***	42.0	55.8***
RACE (N)	2705	1188	1573	541
% Nonwhite	0.9	0.3*	2.0	0.2***
SAT-V (N)	2705	1188	1573	541
$\bar{X}$	594.20	654.32***	616.92	681.74***
SD	82.45	57.85	80.90	51.70
SAT-M (N)	2705	1188	1573	541
$\bar{X}$	636.40	693.30***	609.69	673.82***
SD	79.53	53.93	79.43	51.78

TABLE 6.10   (Continued)

	Males		Females	
	Total Population	Accepted Population	Total Population	Accepted Population
TERMINAL DEGREE PLANS (N)	2700	1186	1572	541
% BA, BS	12.8	7.8***	30.6	22.9***
% MA, MS	23.9	21.1	44.4	48.2
% BD	0.4	0.2	0.1	0.0
% LLB	14.1	14.2	2.3	2.8
% MD	22.9	21.9	9.1	10.2
% PhD, EdD	25.9	34.9	13.5	15.9
PROPOSED MAJOR (N)	2704	1187	1572	540
% Humanities	37.0	32.6***	53.5	51.1
% Social sciences	9.9	12.6	12.0	12.8
% Bio. sciences	25.7	25.9	17.2	16.1
% Physical sciences	27.1	28.6	17.1	19.8
% Other	0.3	0.3	0.2	0.2
CAREER PLANS (N)	2697	1184	1572	540
% Business	16.6	11.1***	5.9	3.9*
% Engineering	1.4	1.4	0.3	0.2
% Law	19.0	18.8	2.7	3.0
% Medicine	23.8	23.1	10.4	10.7
% Politics	3.5	3.5	2.4	1.9
% Science research	14.2	19.9	13.4	16.3
% Education	6.6	8.2	25.7	22.4
% Other	14.8	14.0	39.2	41.7
NMSC RECOGNITION (N)	2705	1188	1573	541
% Recognized	27.0	52.5***	29.7	57.3***
CONVERTED CLASS RANK (N)	2705	1188	1573	541
$\bar{X}$	61.88	66.87***	65.50	71.06***
SD	8.01	6.05	7.48	5.21
OVERALL NONACADEMIC ACCOMPLISHMENTS (N)	2705	1188	1573	541
$\bar{X}$	8.32	8.91***	9.81	10.11*
SD	3.78	3.66	3.57	3.52
LEADERSHIP (N)	2705	1188	1573	541
% Leaders	17.0	18.7*	8.0	8.7
ART (N)	2705	1188	1573	541
% Artists	5.1	3.7**	11.8	10.5
SOCIAL SERVICE (N)	2705	1188	1573	541
% Social service involvement	20.0	19.9	19.9	21.6
WRITING (N)	2705	1188	1573	541
% Writers	9.5	11.3**	14.6	19.2***
EDITING (N)	2705	1188	1573	541
% Editors	12.8	15.8***	21.0	26.6***
DRAMATIC ARTS (N)	2705	1188	1573	541
% Dramatic arts involvement	7.7	9.4**	6.9	6.1
MUSIC (N)	2705	1188	1573	541
% Musicians	12.9	14.1	13.5	13.5

TABLE 6.10   (Continued)

	Males		Females	
	Total Population	Accepted Population	Total Population	Accepted Population
SCIENCE (N)	2705	1188	1573	541
% Science involvement	8.4	12.4***	7.4	9.8**
ATHLETICS (N)	2705	1188	1573	541
% Athletes	16.2	12.1***	5.2	3.7
EMPLOYMENT (N)	2705	1188	1573	541
% Employed	18.7	17.7	4.8	4.1

research and not those planning careers in business (Table 6.10). The actual committee is in essential agreement with the SAT plus rank committee regarding these biases (Table 6.11).

Turning now to accomplishment characteristics, consider first academic forms of accomplishment. Again, as it would have to because of what comprises our decision rule, the class selected by the SAT plus rank committee shows substantially higher grade achievement in high school than the applicant pool (Table 6.10). However, Table 6.11 indicates that in those instances where the actual committee admits students rejected by the SAT plus rank committee, the effect is to lower somewhat the degree of high school grade achievement below what it would be if the SAT plus rank committee had its way on all cases. Fully parallel results obtain with respect to NMSC recognition: heightened proportions of candidates who have received NMSC recognition are found among those accepted by the SAT plus rank committee, and somewhat of a cutback in this regard occurs when we consider the instances where the actual committee and the SAT plus rank committee were in disagreement. Given the nature of NMSC recognition, there is, of course, every reason to expect that it should function in the same manner as SAT scores. And this is exactly what happens.

When it comes to nonacademic accomplishments, Table 6.10 indicates that the actions of the SAT plus rank committee make for small but consistent augmentation effects in the case of overall nonacademic accomplishments and in the case of three of the ten areas that received separate consideration—writing, editing, and science involvement. In terms of number of areas of talented nonacademic attainments and in terms of magnitudes, these effects are quite modest. Does the actual committee, in turn, place greater emphasis on talented nonacademic accomplishments than the SAT plus rank committee? Table 6.11 indicates that there are no statistically significant effects consistent for both

TABLE 6.11   Characteristics of Applicants about Whom There
Was Disagreement between the Admissions Decisions
Made by the Actual Committee and the SAT plus
High School Rank Committee

	Males		Females	
	Actual Comm. Accepts, SAT plus High School Rank Comm. Rejects	Actual Comm. Rejects, SAT plus High School Rank Comm. Accepts	Actual Comm. Accepts, SAT plus High School Rank Comm. Rejects	Actual Comm. Rejects, SAT plus High School Rank Comm. Accepts
PARENT EDUCATION (N)	270	270	155	155
% Non-H.S. graduate	6.7	4.1	3.2	4.5
% H.S. graduate	11.5	12.2	5.2	8.4
% Post-H.S., no degree	15.9	23.0	16.1	22.6
% College graduate	25.6	26.3	31.0	22.6
% Post-college	40.4	34.4	44.5	41.9
SCHOOL TYPE (N)	269	269	155	153
% Public	63.2	81.0***	65.8	92.2***
% Parochial	3.7	5.2	0.6	1.3
% Private	33.1	13.8	33.5	6.5
TYPE OF HOME COMMUNITY (N)	270	270	155	155
% Metropolitan, > 1,000,000	15.6	18.1**	19.4	20.6*
% Suburban, < 1,000,000	6.7	16.3	14.2	20.0
% City, 500,000–1,000,000	2.2	3.3	3.2	1.3
% City, 100,000–500,000	19.6	12.2	14.8	5.8
% City, 10,000–100,000	33.3	33.7	34.8	29.7
% Town, < 10,000	17.4	13.7	10.3	18.1
% Farm or open country	5.2	2.6	3.2	4.5
COMMUNITY ECONOMIC RESOURCES (N)	270	270	155	155
% Agriculture	13.0	5.6***	3.9	7.7
% Heavy industry	5.9	5.9	12.9	7.7
% Light industry	15.6	5.2	12.3	11.0
% Residential	15.9	38.9	21.9	33.5
% Commerce	9.6	9.6	7.7	5.2
% Mining	0.7	0.0	1.3	0.0
% Diversified	39.3	34.8	40.0	34.8
PLACE OF RESIDENCE (N)	270	270	155	155
% Home state	41.5	0.0***	33.5	2.6***
% Regional, not home state	31.9	42.6	28.4	44.5
% Rest of U.S.	24.8	56.7	34.8	52.3
% Foreign	1.9	0.7	3.2	0.6

TABLE 6.11   (Continued)

	Males		Females	
	Actual Comm. Accepts, SAT plus High School Rank Comm. Rejects	Actual Comm. Rejects, SAT plus High School Rank Comm. Accepts	Actual Comm. Accepts, SAT plus High School Rank Comm. Rejects	Actual Comm. Rejects, SAT plus High School Rank Comm. Accepts
PARENT ALUMNI STATUS (N)	270	270	155	155
% Alumni	17.4	0.0***	21.9	0.6***
FINANCIAL AID (N)	270	270	155	155
% Aid applicants	40.4	43.7	37.4	52.3**
RACE (N)	270	270	155	155
% Nonwhite	5.2	0.0***	5.8	0.0**
SAT-V (N)	270	270	155	155
$\bar{X}$	576.84	629.37***	621.66	661.05***
SD	59.54	54.50	59.04	50.10
SAT-M (N)	270	270	155	155
$\bar{X}$	602.24	681.00***	592.69	659.18***
SD	61.99	47.33	62.10	49.35
TERMINAL DEGREE PLANS (N)	270	268	155	155
% BA, BS	14.4	9.7	27.7	20.6
% MA, MS	22.6	23.1	43.2	44.5
% BD	0.0	0.4	0.0	0.0
% LLB	13.7	16.8	2.6	5.2
% MD	27.0	19.8	6.5	10.3
% PhD, EdD	22.2	30.2	20.0	19.4
PROPOSED MAJOR (N)	270	270	155	154
% Humanities	41.1	37.0	60.6	48.1
% Social sciences	9.6	12.6	11.6	15.6
% Bio. sciences	28.1	23.3	12.9	19.5
% Physical sciences	20.4	27.0	14.8	16.2
% Other	0.7	0.0	0.0	0.6
CAREER PLANS (N)	269	268	155	155
% Business	16.7	13.8	6.5	5.2
% Engineering	1.1	1.1	0.0	0.6
% Law	18.6	22.4	2.6	5.2
% Medicine	27.1	22.0	7.1	11.0
% Politics	3.7	3.0	4.5	3.2
% Science research	9.3	14.9	12.9	14.8
% Education	5.2	8.2	32.3	23.9
% Other	18.2	14.6	34.2	36.1
NMSC RECOGNITION (N)	270	270	155	155
% Recognized	13.0	33.3***	29.7	40.6*

TABLE 6.11   (Continued)

	Males		Females	
	Actual Comm. Accepts, SAT plus High School Rank Comm. Rejects	Actual Comm. Rejects, SAT plus High School Rank Comm. Accepts	Actual Comm. Accepts, SAT plus High School Rank Comm. Rejects	Actual Comm. Rejects, SAT plus High School Rank Comm. Accepts
CONVERTED CLASS RANK (N)	270	270	155	155
$\bar{X}$	60.98	63.03***	65.27	69.32***
SD	6.80	5.81	6.83	5.28
OVERALL NONACADEMIC ACCOMPLISHMENTS (N)	270	270	155	155
$\bar{X}$	9.13	8.16**	10.20	9.76
SD	3.85	3.51	3.53	3.72
LEADERSHIP (N)	270	270	155	155
% Leaders	16.7	15.9	7.7	6.5
ART (N)	270	270	155	155
% Artists	7.0	4.4	10.3	13.5
SOCIAL SERVICE (N)	270	270	155	155
% Social service involvement	22.6	17.8	16.8	18.7
WRITING (N)	270	270	155	155
% Writers	15.6	6.3***	12.3	16.1
EDITING (N)	270	270	155	155
% Editors	14.1	12.6	25.8	20.6
DRAMATIC ARTS (N)	270	270	155	155
% Dramatic arts involvement	10.0	8.9	9.7	7.1
MUSIC (N)	270	270	155	155
% Musicians	10.4	11.5	16.1	9.7
SCIENCE (N)	270	270	155	155
% Science involvement	9.3	5.6	8.4	8.4
ATHLETICS (N)	270	270	155	155
% Athletes	19.3	15.9	5.8	2.6
EMPLOYMENT (N)	270	270	155	155
% Employed	14.4	21.5*	3.2	5.8

sexes with respect to any of the 11 variables in question. That is, the modest degree of augmentation concerning nonacademic accomplishment characteristics that results from the actions of the SAT plus rank committee is not countered. But also it is not enhanced as a function of whatever decisions the actual committee makes that disagree with those of the SAT plus rank committee. The SAT plus rank committee, therefore, provides only a small degree of differential emphasis on talented nonacademic attainments relative to their base-rates in the total applicant population, and the actual committee, while it accepts this much emphasis, does not add anything further.

In sum, the SAT plus high school rank committee makes decisions that agree substantially with those of the actual admissions committee. A hypothetical decision rule based only on knowing each applicant's SAT scores and grade rank in high school admits 71 to 77 percent of the same freshman class as does the actual committee. In those cases remaining where the decisions of the two committees disagree, the discrepancies seem mainly to arise because the actual committee somewhat relaxes its reliance on SAT scores and secondary school grades in order to give enhanced weight to certain status characteristics—most notably, residence in the home state of the university, alumni family affiliation, and nonwhite racial background. The actual committee apparently does not give weight to talented nonacademic attainments of applicants beyond the modest degree to which these attainments are already represented in the class chosen by the hypothetical SAT plus high school rank committee.

Conclusions

What have we learned about the workings of the actual admissions committee by comparing its decisions with those of our three hypothetical committees, all of which selected students in terms of one or another definition of academic skills? The actual committee gives strong emphasis to SAT scores and to high school academic achievement in judging the acceptability of its applicants. Nevertheless, the actual committee does admit some students who are less high than they might be in regard to these indices of academic skills, and the major additional characteristics of the students so admitted are home state residence, alumni affiliation, some additional signs of upper socioeconomic status, and nonwhite racial background. The actual committee does not, in turn, seem to make much effort to recognize nonacademic forms of talented attainments—that is, kinds of talents other than those already summarized by intelligence test scores and secondary school grade achievement. We may therefore conclude that actual admissions decisions are governed primarily by a disposition to skim off the cream of the crop with regard to SAT scores and high school grades, while also showing preference for students with a few easily identifiable status characteristics. Our observation is that the actual admissions process fails to grant explicit recognition to a rich diversity of human talents that express themselves in nonacademic ways.

CHAPTER SEVEN

Selecting a Class
for Talented Nonacademic
Accomplishments

The results of our research indicate that talents which candidates display outside the academic arena of intelligence test scores and high school grades have relatively little to do with the decisions made by an actual admissions committee at a typical high-selectivity institution. Our findings have led us to the view that the admissions process at such institutions is based chiefly on a preference for applicants with the highest SAT scores and the best grades in high school, with the additional recognition of a few status characteristics. Yet lip service is widely paid to the desirability of nourishing a wide variety of talents through the admissions policy. Many colleges state flatly that they want students who have demonstrated special talents in such fields of endeavor as creative writing, the visual arts, music, dramatics, and political leadership. Evidently colleges would like to admit students on the basis of broad and diversified definitions of talented attainments, but in actual fact they base their selections on a narrow set of criteria centering upon academic performances. There seems to be therefore a clearly demonstrable gap between what colleges intend in their admissions procedures and what actually takes place.

What could be an alternative? Suppose we postulate a hypothetical committee that explicitly makes its selections on the basis of talented attainments in various fields outside of the traditional academic arena. We will call it the "Nonacademic Accomplishment Committee" and it will accept or reject from among the same total population of applicants considered in Chapters 5 and 6. How different in its membership will the class selected by this hypothetical committee turn out to be from the class that was selected by the actual admissions committee? How will the class selected by the nonacademic accomplishment committee look when compared with the applicant pool? What specific differences in student characteristics will emerge between this kind of class and the class that was actually accepted? What is the relative bearing on a student's actual likelihood of admissions if he is acceptable in the eyes of the nonacademic accomplishment committee as compared to his being acceptable in the eyes of a committee that selects solely for academic skills? These are the questions to which we turn in the present chapter.

As far as we have been able to ascertain, choosing students on the basis of their talented attainments outside the domain of academic skills mirrors very little of the real world of college admissions. We feel that it should come to represent more of what actually goes on. There seem to be few colleges with explicitly defined or explicitly practiced arrangements for showing admissions preference to applicants with strong non-academic attainments. When colleges do try to exhibit this kind of preference, they appear to be making appraisals or forming judgments of candidates on bases that remain highly subjective—bases that are private rather than public. What we were seeking to do in setting up the nonacademic accomplishment committee, on the other hand, was to specify a realistic and explicit policy for admitting students on the basis of their talented attainments in pursuits beyond the classroom. We wanted to define these attainments broadly and diversely, but with sufficient clarity and precision so that our approach would be public and therefore reproducible. To succeed in this would, we believe, constitute a departure from any actual admissions practices of which we are aware, even at those few highly selective colleges where efforts have been made to view talent more broadly.

In more specific terms, our overall objective requires us to fulfill three criteria. First, we must establish an ordering of students in the applicant pool with regard to their talented attainments outside the conventional realm of academic skills, and admit preferentially those who are "most talented" by this definition. Second, we must make sure that applicants representing a number of different areas of talented attainments are admitted, so that genuine diversity of talent will be present in the overall class. Theoretically, we could stop at this point and design the policy of the nonacademic accomplishment committee in such a way that it would meet the two criteria now enumerated. From a practical viewpoint, however, and from an ethical viewpoint as well, a third criterion must be added, and it is this. No matter how talented the candidate may be at nonacademic pursuits, we must set a minimum level of qualifications to be met regarding academic skills—that is, SAT scores and high school grades—before the nonacademic accomplishment committee will accept him. Establishing a "floor" in this manner insures that our hypothetical committee will not admit anyone who would be at a distinct disadvantage in academic terms. The mandate given to the nonacademic accomplishment committee, therefore, is that it must (1) select the "most talented" individuals, (2) assure representation from a number of diverse areas in which talented nonacademic attainments can be demonstrated, and (3) restrict its acceptances to students who are reasonably well qualified academically. Like our other hypothetical committees, the nonacademic accomplishment committee must admit numbers of males and females that are equal to the numbers chosen by the actual committee.

Let us start first with the last of these criteria. How did we define the minimum academic standards that a candidate had to meet before the nonacademic accomplishment committee could consider him? Cut-off points were set regarding SAT scores and high school-grade rank. As to SAT scores, all candidates were rejected whose combined scores on the verbal and mathematical sections of the SAT totaled less than 950. Referring to the College Entrance Examination Board's *Guide for Counselors and Admissions Officers* (College Entrance Examination Board, 1968), which presents separate data for SAT-V and SAT-M scores, we find that a total score of 950 on the SAT approximates the fiftieth percentile for all high school seniors who later entered college. Thus, using 950 as a cutoff score eliminates as academically unqualified those applicants who scored on their SAT's within the lower half of the score range for all high school students who go on to college. We chose this SAT floor because it is widely held that students whose SAT scores are lower than the national average for those who go on to college do not compete well academically in the highly selective colleges. As to rank in high school class, all candidates were rejected who ranked in the bottom third of their secondary school classes—a converted class rank score of less than 47. We chose this grade rank minimum because it has been generally observed that students who are not sufficiently interested in their high school academic work to rank above the lowest third in their class also usually do poorly academically in college. This holds true not only for students in the lowest third at ordinary high schools but also for those in the lowest third at the more competitive and prestigious secondary schools where the SAT score level may be well above the national average.

We turn now to the question of how our first two criteria for the operation of the nonacademic accomplishment committee were fulfilled. Our task was to utilize the assessment information collected from the applicant population concerning talented nonacademic attainments in such a way as to give greater preference to those who are more accomplished. At the same time we had to make sure that all relevant areas of potential accomplishment received adequate representation. Included for consideration were all domains where high-quality attainments would depend at least in part on some form of cognitive capability. These domains were eight in number—leadership, art, social service, writing, editing, dramatic arts, music, and science. Because they did not meet this specification, the areas of athletics and employment were excluded. The eight areas of interest had been shown in our earlier research (Wallach and Wing, 1969) to be independent of general intelligence. Recall also from our discussion of the results for the SAT committee in Chapter 6 that this finding has been replicated in our present research undertaking as well.

Using the same scoring definitions for excellence in each domain taken separately as were presented in Chapter 5, every applicant was evaluated for presence or absence of a significant level of accomplishment in each of the eight categories. A score of "presence" for a domain meant that the candidate had displayed relatively rare accomplishments of a high order of quality in the area in question. In the case of writing, for example, "presence" was scored if the candidate's original writing had been published in a public newspaper, magazine, or anthology (school publications excluded), or if the candidate had won a literary prize for creative writing. With eight domains where a score of "presence" could be earned, the total score for any one candidate could range from no presence scores at all to a theoretical maximum of eight presence scores, one for each domain—that is, from zero to eight. Applicants who obtained a total score of one or higher were listed in *each* accomplishment area where they had scored. In each of these accomplishment areas, the order of listing was set according to the applicant's *total* score—that is, those with the highest total scores were listed first, followed by those with the next highest total scores, and so on. For example, if an applicant had a total score of three, obtained because he had earned presence scores in leadership, social service, and editing, he was listed in all three domains and was placed ahead of all other candidates listed in each of those domains who had achieved totals of two or one. As in selections for the other hypothetical committees, male and female quotas of acceptance were filled separately. Also as before, if ties occurred at the lowest ranking accept position, choices proceeded from the tied ranks at random until the quota was filled.

Acceptance of students proceeded in a carrousel fashion around the eight areas: the most preferred student was chosen for each accomplishment area until all eight areas were represented once, then the next most preferred student in each of the areas was selected, and so on, repeating the process within sex until the acceptance quota for each sex had been filled. Thus, for instance, beginning with the males, the first student accepted was the male who, among all males with leadership scores, had the highest total score. That student was then removed from all other areas in which he had scored. The next student chosen was the male who, among all males with scores in the art domain, had the highest total score. He was then removed from all other areas where he had received scores, and the selection continued until all eight areas were represented with one selection. Then the second round of selection coverage for each of the eight areas began. This procedure insures that only students with significant attainments in at least one of the eight areas were included in the group accepted. At the same time, it gives preference to students with significant accomplishments in larger numbers of areas, and guarantees that all eight areas of potential attainment receive equitable representation in the class accepted for entrance. As an illustration of the area-balancing effect, students whose total score was two and who were listed in the social service category were being drawn at the same time as students with a total score of one and who received that score for excellence in art—thus reflecting the lower incidence of significant art attainments relative to the incidence of significant social service attainments. Our system thus made sure that all eight areas of talented attainments received weight in the accepted class, while also giving as much preference as possible to students who were "most talented"—students with significant attainments in the largest number of areas.

In sum, the nonacademic accomplishment committee pays attention to academic skills, but only to the extent of requiring that intelligence test scores and high school-grade ranks be sufficiently high that the student can be expected to do acceptable academic work in highly selective colleges. Once satisfied on this point, the committee turns to a range of criteria concerning talented nonacademic attainments in deciding upon admissions, assuring representation in the class from a diversity of areas in which humans make meaningful contributions to their world, and giving preference to students who are the most talented in these respects. In terms of the goal of furthering, through one's admissions policy, the full range of ways in which human excellence reveals itself, and furthering the development of those who are most likely to make the strongest contributions to society in these various domains, we feel, on the basis of the kinds of evidence discussed in Chapter 1, that the present type of approach has more to recommend it than one which gives its salient emphasis to SAT scores and high school grades. At the same time, the kinds of assessments that we have conducted for detecting significant talented attainments in nonacademic pursuits, and the technique for carrying out admissions selections once the necessary information is in hand, are explicitly and publicly defined so that they can be reproduced in the admissions activities of any college that cares to replicate the process. Having described it, however, we must turn now to the all-important empirical issue of what this process accomplishes that is different from conventional admissions procedures.

It does a great deal that is different. Table 7.1 indicates the degree of consensus between the decisions of the nonacademic accomplishment committee and the actual committee. Keep in mind first of all that the nonacademic accomplishment committee required a certain level of academic credentials as part of the basis for its selection, so that we know in advance that both committees will tend to reject the lowest candidates as to SAT scores and secondary school grades. This factor will work, of course, toward raising the level of agreement between the two committees. Despite the point just mentioned, what we find from Table 7.1 is that the extent of agreement between the nonacademic accomplishment committee and the actual committee is far lower than that between any of the academic skills-oriented hypothetical committees and the actual committee. A hypothetical committee choosing in terms of talented nonacademic accomplishments and the actual committee disagree very substantially indeed.

Consider first the error-reduction index values. If we try to predict the actual committee's decisions from those of the nonacademic accomplishment committee, we reduce the chance rate of error only 17.3 percent for males and 11.3 percent for females. Compare these figures with 59.5 percent for males and 56.3 percent for females when using the deci-

TABLE 7.1   Extent of Decisional Agreement between the Actual Committee and the Nonacademic Accomplishment Committee

Actual Committee Admissions Decisions		Nonacademic Accomplishment Committee Admissions Decisions					
		Males			Females		
		Accept	Reject	Total Observed	Accept	Reject	Total Observed
Accept {	Observed	637	551	1188	226	315	541
	Expected	522	666		186	355	
Reject {	Observed	551	966	1517	315	717	1032
	Expected	666	851		355	677	
Total observed				2705			1673

Predictive Accuracy	Males	Females
Error-reduction index	17.3	11.3
% Decisions in agreement	59.3	59.9
% Acceptances in agreement	53.6	41.8

sions of the SAT plus high school rank committee as the basis for predicting what the actual committee will do. Regarding the percentage of all decisions that are in agreement between the nonacademic accomplishment and the actual committees, the figures are 59.3 percent for males and 59.9 percent for females. By comparison, these numbers were 80 percent for males and 80.3 percent for females when considering the percentage of decisions in agreement between the SAT plus rank committee and the actual committee. Turning finally to the percentage of acceptances that are in agreement between the nonacademic accomplishment and the actual committees, there are only 53.6 percent of male acceptances and 41.8 percent of female acceptances that agree. Compare these percentages with 77.3 percent acceptance decisions for males and 71.3 percent acceptance decisions for females that are in agreement between the SAT plus rank committee and the actual committee.

What these last comparisons signify is that while about 70 or 80 percent of the class chosen by the SAT plus rank committee is the same as that chosen by the actual committee, only about 40 or 50 percent of the class chosen by the nonacademic accomplishment committee is the same as that chosen by the actual committee. Thus, the nonacademic accomplishment committee selects a class that is about 50 to 60 percent different in its composition from the actual class. That is a striking degree of difference in class membership, and particularly so when we realize that the SAT plus rank committee selects a class that is only about 20 or 30 percent different in its membership from the actual class. In spite of the inclusion of certain academic skills requirements in the policy of the nonacademic accomplishment committee, the latter selects a class that is very different from the actual class.

Against the background of this relatively low agreement between the actions of the nonacademic accomplishment committee and the actual committee, let us examine the characteristics of the nonacademic accomplishment committee's class. Table 7.2 compares it with the applicant population, while Table 7.3 considers the ways in which it differs from the class actually chosen. We turn first to status attributes. Table 7.2 reveals that there are no consistent status biases one way or another for the nonacademic accomplishment committee's class, except that those applying for financial aid receive a certain degree of preference. In regard to the other seven status characteristics, however, the nonacademic accomplishment committee accepts a class that is comparable to the applicant pool. Consistent disagreement on the part of the actual committee as to status characteristics occurs (Table 7.3) in its favoring of those from the home state and those with alumni affiliations, and its even greater favoring of financial aid applicants than was the case for the nonacademic accomplishment committee. This last point indicates

TABLE 7.2   Characteristics of Total Applicant Population
and of Population Accepted by the Nonacademic
Accomplishment Committee

	Males		Females	
	Total Population	Accepted Population	Total Population	Accepted Population
PARENT EDUCATION (N)	2705	1188	1573	541
% Non-H.S. graduate	4.4	4.2	4.6	4.8
% H.S. graduate	10.7	10.9	8.5	8.7
% Post-H.S., no degree	20.3	19.4	19.6	19.8
% College graduate	28.8	27.9	26.7	29.0
% Post-college	35.8	37.6	40.6	37.7
SCHOOL TYPE (N)	2700	1186	1567	540
% Public	72.9	77.4***	79.1	78.3
% Parochial	4.3	3.6	2.4	2.4
% Private	22.8	19.0	18.5	19.3
TYPE OF HOME COMMUNITY (N)	2703	1187	1569	541
% Metropolitan, > 1,000,000	15.6	13.8*	18.0	17.4
% Suburban, < 1,000,000	17.6	17.1	17.9	15.3
% City, 500,000–1,000,000	2.2	1.6	2.7	2.2
% City, 100,000–500,000	14.1	14.3	12.4	11.8
% City, 10,000–100,000	32.3	33.1	32.4	32.7
% Town, < 10,000	13.9	15.7	11.9	14.4
% Farm or open country	4.3	4.4	4.7	6.1
COMMUNITY ECONOMIC RESOURCES (N)	2701	1185	1570	541
% Agriculture	7.9	9.1**	6.2	7.2
% Heavy industry	7.6	6.8	8.6	7.8
% Light industry	10.0	11.2	11.1	11.8
% Residential	30.9	28.2	29.5	27.9
% Commerce	7.6	6.8	6.4	8.1
% Mining	0.4	0.8	0.6	0.4
% Diversified	35.6	37.1	37.6	36.8
PLACE OF RESIDENCE (N)	2704	1188	1572	541
% Home state	10.5	11.4*	13.0	14.4
% Regional, not home state	37.8	40.5	38.7	38.3
% Rest of U.S.	50.4	47.0	46.1	44.7
% Foreign	1.3	1.2	2.1	2.6
PARENT ALUMNI STATUS (N)	2704	1188	1572	541
% Alumni	4.9	5.0	7.1	7.0
FINANCIAL AID (N)	2705	1188	1573	541
% Aid applicants	39.6	45.5***	42.0	46.2*
RACE (N)	2705	1188	1573	541
% Nonwhite	0.9	0.6	2.0	2.0
SAT-V (N)	2705	1188	1573	541
$\bar{X}$	594.20	605.67***	616.92	632.94***
SD	82.45	78.60	80.90	69.39
SAT-M (N)	2705	1188	1573	541
$\bar{X}$	636.40	645.21***	609.69	615.83*
SD	79.53	74.71	79.43	74.09

TABLE 7.2   (Continued)

	Males		Females	
	Total Population	Accepted Population	Total Population	Accepted Population
TERMINAL DEGREE PLANS (N)	2700	1186	1572	540
% BA, BS	12.8	8.5***	30.6	23.9***
% MA, MS	23.9	20.3	44.4	46.1
% BD	0.4	0.3	0.1	0.0
% LLB	14.1	15.1	2.3	3.1
% MD	22.9	24.7	9.1	10.9
% PhD, EdD	25.9	31.1	13.5	15.9
PROPOSED MAJOR (N)	2704	1187	1572	541
% Humanities	37.0	36.6***	53.5	54.5*
% Social sciences	9.9	11.6	12.0	10.5
% Bio. sciences	25.7	28.0	17.2	20.5
% Physical sciences	27.1	23.5	17.1	14.2
% Other	0.3	0.3	0.2	0.2
CAREER PLANS (N)	2697	1184	1572	541
% Business	16.6	13.2***	5.9	4.4**
% Engineering	1.4	0.7	0.3	0.2
% Law	19.0	20.8	2.7	4.3
% Medicine	23.8	25.4	10.4	12.6
% Politics	3.5	4.2	2.4	2.2
% Science research	14.2	14.1	13.4	14.4
% Education	6.6	7.9	25.7	21.4
% Other	14.8	13.7	39.2	40.5
NMSC RECOGNITION (N)	2705	1188	1573	541
% Recognized	27.0	31.6***	29.7	33.6*
CONVERTED CLASS RANK (N)	2705	1188	1573	541
$\bar{X}$	61.88	64.03***	65.50	66.92***
SD	8.01	7.05	7.48	6.73
OVERALL NONACADEMIC ACCOMPLISHMENTS (N)	2705	1188	1573	541
$\bar{X}$	8.32	10.39***	9.81	12.22***
SD	3.78	3.36	3.57	3.17
LEADERSHIP (N)	2705	1188	1573	541
% Leaders	17.0	31.6***	8.0	15.3***
ART (N)	2705	1188	1573	541
% Artists	5.1	9.3***	11.8	27.0***
SOCIAL SERVICE (N)	2705	1188	1573	541
% Social service involvement	20.0	36.9***	19.9	40.1***
WRITING (N)	2705	1188	1573	541
% Writers	9.5	19.3***	14.6	33.8***
EDITING (N)	2705	1188	1573	541
% Editors	12.8	24.6***	21.0	42.3***
DRAMATIC ARTS (N)	2705	1188	1573	541
% Dramatic arts involvement	7.7	14.8***	6.9	15.7***
MUSIC (N)	2705	1188	1573	541
% Musicians	12.9	24.6***	13.5	26.8***

TABLE 7.2   (Continued)

	Males		Females	
	Total Population	Accepted Population	Total Population	Accepted Population
SCIENCE (N)	2705	1188	1573	541
% Science involvement	8.4	15.6***	7.4	15.5***
ATHLETICS (N)	2705	1188	1573	541
% Athletes	16.2	15.6	5.2	6.1
EMPLOYMENT (N)	2705	1188	1573	541
% Employed	18.7	19.8	4.8	4.8

that in accepting financial aid applicants, the actual committee looks to some extent elsewhere than to the candidates accepted by the non-academic accomplishment committee. The home state and alumni affiliation preferences of the actual committee, in turn, indicate once more the differentially greater acceptability to the actual committee of "home team" students.

Of particular interest in the area of status characteristics is the comparability of racial makeup between the class chosen by the nonacademic accomplishment committee and the applicant pool. The nonacademic accomplishment committee turns out to choose whites and nonwhites in about the same proportions as they occur in the applicant population (Table 7.2). This finding contrasts with the effects produced by the actions of the SAT committee which rejected all except one nonwhite (Table 6.2). Selecting students on the basis of nonacademic accomplishments thus seems to discriminate against nonwhites less than does a selection procedure based upon SAT scores. However, selecting students on the basis of their high school ranks was found to actually favor nonwhites relative to their proportion in the applicant population (Table 6.5). Consideration of secondary school grade ranks and of nonacademic attainments, therefore, provide approaches to defining merit that seem to be less biased against nonwhites than is the case for consideration of SAT scores.

This conclusion receives further support when we turn to the cases of disagreement between the actual committee and the various hypothetical committees. The actual committee, in its choice discrepancies from particular hypothetical committees, favored nonwhites more than the SAT committee in the case of both sexes (Table 6.3); favored nonwhites less than the high school rank committee in the case of females but was comparable in the case of males (Table 6.6); and favored non-

TABLE 7.3   Characteristics of Applicants about Whom There Was Disagreement between the Admissions Decisions Made by the Actual Committee and the Non-academic Accomplishment Committee

	Males		Females	
	Actual Comm. Accepts, Nonacademic Accom. Comm. Rejects	Actual Comm. Rejects, Nonacademic Accom. Comm. Accepts	Actual Comm. Accepts, Nonacademic Accom. Comm. Rejects	Actual Comm. Rejects, Nonacademic Accom. Comm. Accepts
PARENT EDUCATION (N)	551	551	315	315
% Non-H.S. graduate	5.4	5.1	3.5	5.7
% H.S. graduate	9.8	10.7	6.7	8.9
% Post-H.S., no degree	20.1	20.9	18.4	22.9
% College graduate	26.9	27.4	28.3	22.5
% Post-college	37.7	35.9	43.2	40.0
SCHOOL TYPE (N)	549	550	314	315
% Public	75.8	74.5	77.1	77.5
% Parochial	2.7	5.2	1.3	2.5
% Private	21.5	20.2	21.7	20.0
TYPE OF HOME COMMUNITY (N)	550	550	315	315
% Metropolitan, > 1,000,000	16.2	11.5***	20.6	21.3
% Suburban, < 1,000,000	15.1	20.2	14.9	14.9
% City, 500,000–1,000,000	2.2	2.0	3.5	2.5
% City, 100,000–500,000	17.6	10.2	12.4	9.2
% City, 10,000–100,000	30.5	34.2	34.9	32.1
% Town, < 10,000	13.6	16.5	9.2	13.7
% Farm or open country	4.7	5.5	4.4	6.3
COMMUNITY ECONOMIC RESOURCES (N)	550	551	315	315
% Agriculture	8.4	9.6*	5.1	8.6
% Heavy industry	8.0	7.8	9.5	7.3
% Light industry	9.1	9.8	10.8	11.4
% Residential	28.5	34.7	27.3	27.9
% Commerce	6.4	4.9	6.0	7.6
% Mining	0.0	0.7	0.6	0.0
% Diversified	39.6	32.5	40.6	37.1
PLACE OF RESIDENCE (N)	550	551	315	315
% Home state	20.2	2.7***	21.9	7.6***
% Regional, not home state	37.3	39.6	36.8	40.3
% Rest of U.S.	41.3	56.4	39.7	49.2
% Foreign	1.3	1.3	1.6	2.9

TABLE 7.3   (Continued)

	Males		Females	
	Actual Comm. Accepts, Nonacademic Accom. Comm. Rejects	Actual Comm. Rejects, Nonacademic Accom. Comm. Accepts	Actual Comm. Accepts, Nonacademic Accom. Comm. Rejects	Actual Comm. Rejects, Nonacademic Accom. Comm. Accepts
PARENT ALUMNI STATUS (N)	551	551	315	315
% Alumni	8.9	1.5***	12.4	4.1***
FINANCIAL AID (N)	551	551	315	315
% Aid applicants	48.8	34.1***	52.1	42.9*
RACE (N)	551	551	315	315
% Nonwhite	2.0	0.0***	1.0	1.3
SAT-V (N)	551	551	315	315
$\bar{X}$	640.27	561.12***	669.57	605.12***
SD	66.52	64.98	62.59	62.57
SAT-M (N)	551	551	315	315
$\bar{X}$	676.15	611.06***	656.23	589.36***
SD	69.04	65.34	67.17	66.71
TERMINAL DEGREE PLANS (N)	551	549	315	314
% BA, BS	11.8	11.1	27.9	26.1
% MA, MS	24.0	22.6	46.7	43.6
% BD	0.2	0.5	0.0	0.0
% LLB	13.1	16.6	1.6	3.5
% MD	22.3	24.8	8.9	12.1
% PhD, EdD	28.7	24.4	14.9	14.6
PROPOSED MAJOR (N)	551	551	315	315
% Humanities	33.0	39.6*	54.0	53.7***
% Social sciences	11.1	10.5	11.7	9.8
% Bio. sciences	25.2	27.2	12.7	23.5
% Physical sciences	30.3	22.5	21.6	12.7
% Other	0.4	0.2	0.0	0.3
CAREER PLANS (N)	550	549	314	315
% Business	13.6	16.8***	5.4	5.7
% Engineering	2.2	0.5	0.0	0.3
% Law	17.5	23.7	1.0	4.4
% Medicine	23.1	25.7	8.9	14.0
% Politics	2.7	3.8	2.9	2.9
% Science research	20.2	10.4	15.6	13.3
% Education	4.9	5.8	25.2	19.4
% Other	15.8	13.3	41.1	40.0
NMSC RECOGNITION (N)	551	551	315	315
% Recognized	46.6	11.6***	52.4	17.1***

TABLE 7.3   (Continued)

	Males		Females	
	Actual Comm. Accepts, Nonacademic Accom. Comm. Rejects	Actual Comm. Rejects, Nonacademic Accom. Comm. Accepts	Actual Comm. Accepts, Nonacademic Accom. Comm. Rejects	Actual Comm. Rejects, Nonacademic Accom. Comm. Accepts
CONVERTED CLASS RANK (N)	551	551	315	315
$\bar{X}$	65.50	60.39***	69.64	64.51***
SD	6.92	6.12	6.72	6.37
OVERALL NONACADEMIC ACCOMPLISHMENTS (N)	551	551	315	315
$\bar{X}$	7.35	10.07***	8.73	12.13***
SD	3.30	3.35	2.96	3.29
LEADERSHIP (N)	551	551	315	315
% Leaders	5.6	33.2***	4.4	15.2***
ART (N)	551	551	315	315
% Artists	1.5	12.3***	1.9	31.7***
SOCIAL SERVICE (N)	551	551	315	315
% Social service involvement	5.6	39.7***	7.3	40.0***
WRITING (N)	551	551	315	315
% Writers	2.7	15.4***	4.4	31.4***
EDITING (N)	551	551	315	315
% Editors	3.4	21.6***	14.0	38.4***
DRAMATIC ARTS (N)	551	551	315	315
% Dramatic arts involvement	1.5	12.5***	2.5	17.8***
MUSIC (N)	551	551	315	315
% Musicians	2.5	25.8***	5.7	25.4***
SCIENCE (N)	551	551	315	315
% Science involvement	4.5	9.6**	4.1	14.0***
ATHLETICS (N)	551	551	315	315
% Athletes	13.1	18.9**	3.8	6.3
EMPLOYMENT (N)	551	551	315	315
% Employed	14.7	22.7***	4.1	6.7

whites more than the nonacademic accomplishment committee in the
case of males but was comparable in the case of females (Table 7.3).
Hence we see that the actual committee, when it admits nonwhites, has
to underplay SAT scores for both sexes—something it does not have to
do with grades for either sex and has to do with nonacademic attainments
only for males.

Now let us consider personal characteristics. The class selected by
the nonacademic accomplishment committee shows a modest augmentation of SAT scores relative to the applicant pool (Table 7.2). This is
hardly surprising, however, since the nonacademic accomplishment committee builds in a modest enhancement effect for SAT scores by eliminating those students whose SAT scores are below a certain minimum. From
Table 7.3 we see in turn that a major area of disagreement between the
actual committee and the nonacademic accomplishment committee concerns how much emphasis to put on SAT scores. For those applicants
on whom the two committees disagree, the students favored by the actual
committee have far higher SAT scores than the students favored by the
nonacademic accomplishment committee. What this means, of course,
for the considerable number of applicants about whom the two committees disagree, is that the actual committee is admitting students
with high SAT scores but little by way of talented nonacademic attainments, while the nonacademic accomplishment committee is admitting
students with strong nonacademic accomplishments but relatively low
SAT scores—low enough to eventuate in rejection at the hands of the
actual committee.

When we look at the terminal degree plans of the candidates as shown
in Tables 7.2 and 7.3, the actual and the nonacademic accomplishment
committees turn out to agree in selecting classes that incline toward long-
range educational goals rather than toward a terminal bachelor's degree.
While so different in its degree of emphasis on SAT scores and high school
grades from the actual committee, then, the nonacademic accomplishment committee shares the actual committee's preference for students
with long-range educational objectives. It is unlikely, therefore, that the
nonacademic accomplishment committee selects students who are more
frivolous or less serious than those chosen by the actual committee.
As to how these plans are reflected in proposed majors, the class chosen
by the nonacademic accomplishment committee tends to be relatively
more interested in the biological sciences and less interested in the
physical sciences than the applicant pool (Table 7.2). Also, in its disagreements with the selections made by the actual committee, the nonacademic accomplishment committee favors students planning to major in
a biological science and is less favorable toward those proposing physical
science majors (Table 7.3). In line with these effects, the nonacademic

accomplishment committee's class shows a consistent emphasis on career plans in medicine. Law is also consistently emphasized (Table 7.2). While there are no consistent disagreements in these regards from the class chosen by the actual committee, Table 7.3 does indicate that more emphasis is placed on law and medicine for males by the nonacademic accomplishment committee than by the actual committee, and comparable trends—although not reaching statistical significance—are shown for females. As to the broad area of attitudes and values, longer range educational goals seem to characterize the class chosen by the nonacademic accomplishment committee and the class chosen by the actual committee, with the possibility in the former of stronger medical-biological, and weaker physical science interests than in the latter.

Turning next to accomplishment characteristics, let us consider academic attainments—namely, NMSC recognition and rank in high school class. As we would expect, these attributes yield results that parallel what was found for SAT scores. Table 7.2 reveals modest but consistent enhancement regarding both NMSC recognition and high school grade achievement for the class selected by the nonacademic accomplishment committee relative to the applicant pool, and Table 7.3 indicates that the actual committee gives still more weight to both of these factors than does the nonacademic accomplishment committee. Given the link between NMSC recognition and SAT-like assessment, we can expect the requirement of an SAT minimum, by the nonacademic accomplishment committee, to enhance the level of NMSC recognition to a marginal degree as well as to enhance SAT scores in the class it selects. This, of course, is not enough to suit the actual committee. Since the nonacademic accomplishment committee also eliminated from consideration all students whose high school grade ranks were below a certain minimum, it selected a class with modestly but consistently augmented grade ranks relative to the applicant pool. The actual committee, however, wanted its class to have still higher grade ranks. For academic accomplishments as well as for SAT scores, then, the actual committee selected a class with much stronger credentials than the class selected by the nonacademic accomplishment committee—even though the latter committee's class was slightly more qualified in these respects than the applicant pool as a whole. What is the picture, however, in the realm of talented nonacademic attainments?

When it comes to talented accomplishments in nonacademic domains, Table 7.2 indicates that the class selected by a hypothetical committee whose explicit intent it was to search for such attainments does indeed contain large numbers of students who display them. Turning first to the index of overall nonacademic accomplishments, the mean score increases for those accepted are comparable, relative to the applicant pool standard deviations, to the enhancements found regarding SAT scores and high school ranks when the academically oriented committees of Chapter 6 were selecting the class. The proportions of class members with high-level nonacademic accomplishments in the areas of leadership, art, social service, writing, editing, dramatic arts, music, and science, are, in the case of both sexes, way above the proportions found for the applicant population as a whole. The general effect, in fact, is that these proportions tend to double: they are approximately twice as high in the admitted class relative to their levels in the applicant pool. Not only do they double but the proportions in question are sizable ones. For example, substantial attainments in the domain of creative writing were shown, among males, by 9.5 percent of the applicant pool but by 19.3 percent of the admitted class; and among females, by 14.6 percent of the applicant pool but by 33.8 percent of the admitted class. As another illustration, attainments of a high order of quality in the area of art were shown, among males, by 5.1 percent of the applicant pool but by 9.3 percent of the admitted class; and among females, by 11.8 percent of the applicant pool but by 27 percent of the admitted class. This is a class of students who, in large numbers and in substantial degrees, have exhibited excellence in a wide range of life pursuits, extending from leadership in relation to their peers, to attainments in all the major domains of the arts, and also to accomplishments in scientific work. Regarding athletics and employment—kinds of nonacademic attainments from which our hypothetical committee did not select because of their greater remove from issues of a cognitive sort—we note from Table 7.2 that the incidence of the latter types of attainments among the members of the accepted class is comparable to their incidence in the applicant pool.

Consider now in Table 7.3 the nonacademic accomplishment characteristics of the substantial number of applicants who are treated differently by the two committees. Those favored by the actual committee are seldom distinguished in their nonacademic pursuits, while those favored by the nonacademic accomplishment committee—as expected from that committee's orientation—are always more distinguished in these ways. Recalling the qualifications of these respective groups in regard to SAT scores and high school grades, we can guess the source of the frequently encountered disagreements between these two committees. The actual committee is willing to tolerate an absence of distinguished accomplishments outside the classroom if the applicant's SAT scores and academic grades are high enough, while the nonacademic accomplishment committee is willing to tolerate relatively low SAT scores and grades if the applicant has distinguished himself or herself in talented nonacademic pursuits. The consequence of these different outlooks is the selection by the two committees of two quite different freshman classes.

We can now put into perspective what we have learned in the last three chapters. On the one hand, we have presented evidence documenting the close agreement between admissions decisions made by hypothetical committees concerned with academic skills and those made by the actual committee. And on the other hand, we have presented evidence indicating considerably less agreement between the decisions made by the actual committee and the admissions decisions made by a hypothetical committee concerned with talented nonacademic attainments. It should follow that the decisions made by the hypothetical committees that select on the basis of academic skills are substantially different from those made by the hypothetical committee that selects for talented nonacademic accomplishments. We have made such comparisons and found that the results are similar to those obtained when comparing the actual committee with the nonacademic accomplishment committee. What the actual committee does is best described by models that take into account the SAT scores and high school grade ranks of the applicants. It would be poorly described by a model that relies mainly on the talented nonacademic attainments of the applicants.

A straightforward comparison of acceptance likelihoods can be set up which will make this point very clear. Table 7.4 indicates the likelihood of a candidate's acceptance by the actual committee as a function of the decisions made about him by each of two hypothetical committees. One committee selects for academic skills and the other selects for talented nonacademic accomplishments. Of the three academically oriented hypothetical committees that we devised, we utilize here the

TABLE 7.4   Probability of Acceptance by Actual Committee
as a Function of Acceptance versus Rejection by
Nonacademic Accomplishment Committee and by
SAT plus High School Rank Committee

Hypothetical Admissions Decisions		Males			Females		
SAT plus High School Rank Comm.	Nonacademic Accomplishment Committee	Total population	Actual Committee accept population	% accepted by Actual Committee from each decision category	Total population	Actual Committee accept population	% accepted by Actual Committee from each decision category
Accept	Accept	608	504	82.9	218	168	77.1
Accept	Reject	580	414	71.4	323	218	67.5
Reject	Accept	580	133	22.9	323	58	18.0
Reject	Reject	937	137	14.6	709	97	13.7
	Total	2705	1188	43.9	1573	541	34.4

one that was most accurate in predicting the actions of the actual committee—namely, the SAT plus high school rank committee. The other hypothetical committee is the one developed in the present chapter. Again, the results for males and females are presented separately, and they turn out to be parallel. The table divides the applicants into subsets defined by their acceptance or rejection by the SAT plus rank committee and by the nonacademic accomplishment committee. This gives us, within sex, four subsets in all: those rejected by both hypothetical committees, those accepted by one but rejected by the other, and those accepted by both. The table then records how many members of each subset were accepted by the actual committee. Dividing this number by the size of the subset indicates what percentage of the subset's members were actually accepted, and therefore the probability of acceptance by the actual committee as a function of membership in a particular subset. The results of carrying out this division are entered as a percentage figure for each subset.

Table 7.4 shows that of the applicants rejected by both hypothetical committees, only 14.6 percent of the males and 13.7 percent of the females are accepted by the actual committee. These figures represent a base-rate indicating the likelihood of a candidate's acceptance on grounds other than those defined by the policies of either of the two hypothetical committees. This base-rate is about 14 percent. Presumably, it is accounted for in part by such status characteristics as home-state residence and alumni affiliation, in part because of other characteristics, and in part because of unreliability in the actual committee's decision-making process. Let us now examine what acceptance under the rules of each of the two hypothetical committees contributes over this base-rate to the candidate's actual chances of acceptance at the hands of the real committee. If the candidate is acceptable to the nonacademic accomplishment committee but is not acceptable to the SAT plus rank committee, then the probability of actual acceptance increases only a little over the 14 percent base-rate: it goes up to 22.9 percent for the men and 18 percent for the women. On the other hand, if a candidate is acceptable to the SAT plus rank committee but is not acceptable to the nonacademic accomplishment committee the likelihood of acceptance shoots up dramatically to 71.4 percent for the men and 67.5 percent for the women. This is a huge increase over the 14 percent base-rate. Thus, while acceptability by the rules of the nonacademic accomplishment committee but not by the rules of the SAT plus rank committee increases a candidate's likelihood of actual acceptance much less than even one-fold, acceptability by the rules of the SAT plus rank committee but not by the rules of the nonacademic accomplishment committee increases the probability of his actual acceptance almost fivefold.

The maximum increase in likelihood of actual acceptance over the base-rate is found, of course, for those candidates who are acceptable both to the SAT plus rank and to the nonacademic accomplishment committees. For such candidates, the likelihood of actual acceptance is 82.9 percent for the men and 77.1 percent for the women. Note, however, that this actual acceptance likelihood is only slightly higher for the candidates who are acceptable to both hypothetical committees than it is for the candidates who are acceptable to the SAT plus rank committee alone. Thus, the increase in likelihood of actual acceptance over the base-rate is slightly more than five-and-a-half-fold for candidates accepted by both hypothetical committees, but already was almost fivefold for candidates accepted by the SAT plus rank committee but rejected by the nonacademic accomplishment committee. Once again, then, we see that talented nonacademic attainments add by themselves only small increments to the likelihood of actual acceptance. What really counts as far as the actual committee is concerned is SAT scores and grades.

We have been able to document yet again that students identified as talented on the basis of their attainments in various realms outside the conventional academic arena of intelligence test scores and high school grades are only slightly more in demand by an actual admissions committee than students who are not so identified. The actual admissions process is found mainly to depend on SAT scores and high school grade achievement. What the findings of the present chapter tell us in addition, however, is that a realistic alternative to the aforementioned emphasis does in fact exist. We have found that selection for talented nonacademic accomplishments is quite different from selection for intelligence test scores and grades. We have also found that it is not merely a utopian ideal but is quite practical to carry out. A realistic basis for emphasizing a variety of talented nonacademic accomplishments in one's admissions approach—realistic in that it still requires the candidate to meet certain academic skills criteria—has been developed and applied to an applicant population. The result is a class whose membership differs in substantial degree—by some 50 to 60 percent—from the class admitted by the actual committee, and whose membership represents a wide spectrum of distinguished contributions outside the academic sphere. We have shown that selecting a class for talented nonacademic accomplishments can be done in a practical way and makes a genuine difference in the composition of the class that results. But why should one base decisions on these additional selection criteria rather than limit oneself to those customarily in use? Why should one *want* to diversify the grounds for selection?

The answers to these questions take us back, of course, to what was discussed in Chapter 1. Within the upper ranges of academic skills under consideration, differences regarding intellective ability test scores and grades do not seem to have much relation to directly meaningful criteria of attainments in real life, whether looked at contemporaneously or in terms of what the individual goes on to do after completing his schooling. Talented nonacademic accomplishments as we have defined them, on the other hand, are of direct value in their own right as forms of excellence which the society should be interested in supporting. Such accomplishments may also suggest what we might expect from the individual later on. They are in any case the best current demonstrations of intrinsically valuable contributions by the student to his real environment. It is hard to understand therefore why information about these or similar types of attainments should not receive substantial weight in college admissions.

CHAPTER EIGHT

Some Concluding Observations

The general significance of what use our society makes of its talent resources hardly needs emphasis. As Gardner (1961) has noted, it is the particular concern of a free society to provide the opportunity for each individual to develop fully his own capacities. Wolfle (1960), outlining some of the pivotal problems of talent cultivation faced by a modern democracy, has argued that each member of the society ideally should be helped to concentrate his efforts upon the type of endeavor for which his talent is greatest, thus making for maximum diversity in the activities pursued by different individuals. But this is not what is encouraged by current college admissions practices. As the press for access to high selectivity colleges and universities in this country becomes ever greater, so too does the need to understand admissions practices, what effects they have, what has made them the way they are, and what changes could be made.

There appear to be at least three major reasons why admissions practices at the nation's more prestigious institutions of higher learning are important to the development and utilization of our human talent resources. Two of these reasons concern what happens to which students during and after college attendance, and we have discussed them already earlier in the volume. Thus, we considered in Chapters 1 and 4 how admissions practices influence the society's overall direction by selectively helping and hindering the progress of students with particular talents. As a result of these filtration effects, the talents in question take on greater or lesser importance in the culture as a whole. For example, if talents in the visual arts tend to be ignored in admissions decisions, students excelling in that field of endeavor will have less access to the educational opportunities that would serve to develop their potential to make artistic contributions. They also will be less likely as adults to be in a position to maintain and foster a concern for visual esthetics in the society as a whole. The consequences of such effects are apparent. We need look no further than at the ugliness and monotony of the nearest shopping center or suburban sprawl.

In Chapter 4 we also pointed out, as a second reason for the influence of admissions practices, that students learn a great deal from each other during the college years—perhaps even more than they learn from their instructors. To the degree that students at any college are different from one another in the sense of representing a diversity of talents, rather than homogeneous in the sense of possessing the same rarefied levels of academic skills (as the major characteristics distinguishing them from the applicants who were rejected) greater learning increments will result from their spending four years in the same environment. Besides learning more from each other, they will be less prone to the commonly experienced problem of being forced, somewhat irrationally, to view one another as relatively higher or lower performers on the conventional academic skills continuum. For in those terms all of them are adequately qualified in the first place. They will be able to see each other as reflecting different competences from all of which there is something worth learning.

There is in addition a third implication involved in college admissions practices at the high selectivity institutions. This is the one that points toward earlier steps in the schooling sequence rather than toward college and beyond. We propose that realistic hopes for liberalizing the nature of primary and secondary school education are tied in part to the achievement of reforms in college admissions criteria.

It is inevitable that a strong determinant of what primary and secondary school education are like is provided by the character of the entrance requirements to the more prestigious institutions of higher education. To the extent that these requirements emphasize small differentiations within the upper sector of the score distribution on intelligence tests, and small increments within the upper range on grades awarded for assimilating maximal amounts of traditional academic curriculum materials, strong pressure exists below the point of college entrance to concentrate on preparing youngsters to do well on that sort of test and to earn higher grades on that sort of pedagogical fare. Teachers and school administrators quite naturally feel a primary duty to prepare their students as thoroughly as possible for the college admissions hurdle, and parents of course insist that the schools devote major pedagogical attention to whatever is necessary for admission to the highly selective colleges. The basic orientation of primary and secondary school education is therefore heavily influenced by the nature of college admissions requirements. If encouraging the broadening and reforming of primary and secondary school curricula is to be as convincing and effective as possible, serious changes must take place in the requirements for getting into the more prestigious colleges.

Changes of the kinds that we have advocated can, by the same token, be expected to energize a beneficial ripple of changes at earlier levels of the educational sequence, since it would then become reasonable and realistic for educators to encourage those below college age to carry out real-life manifestations of their talents, and for educators to bring such activities within a widened and diversified definition of what education in elementary and high schools is all about. What we would like to see happen in elementary and secondary schools as well as in colleges is a transformation of school into a societal institution that is more representative of the full spectrum of talented pursuits that characterize real-life functioning, and less deformed in the direction of rewarding a narrow range of verbal and quantitative manipulatory skills as the main competences as far as educational advancement is concerned. We would like to reach the point, in other words, where those forms of talented attainments that are categorized as "nonacademic" within the present scheme of things come to be embraced within the academic—within that which is considered worthy and important enough to be part of what formal education concerns.

It is apparent, therefore, that the selection filters comprised by college admissions criteria have consequences for earlier levels of schooling as well as providing differential access to further educational opportunities. College admissions practices influence the goals toward which pedagogy and curricula at earlier educational levels are aimed because such earlier education inevitably moulds itself in substantial degree toward maximizing the likelihood that students will receive the most favorable opportunities to obtain further educational advancement. To recommend, as Bruner (1960; 1966), Jones (1968), Holt (1969), and others have done, changes in precollege teaching practices directed toward a greater emphasis on imagination, on inventiveness, on ingenuity, and on topics of strong natural interest to the students, seems very desirable indeed as a direction of pedagogical reform. As Jones (1968) puts it, ". . . our educational practices have unfortunately developed intrinsic postures of dourness with respect to what really matters to children— what excites, bemuses, and impassions them. This is why school is typically so boring." (p. 245.) He goes on to recommend approaches that would serve, for instance, to encourage expression of imaginativeness as a central pedagogical concern of the school—not as a peripheral activity taught in the manner of a relief from "serious" work by an itinerant outsider who comes in once a week to spend a little time on music, or art, or dramatics, or rhythmic dancing. What Jones wants to see ". . . is something a little closer to the curricular vest, and conducted by the teacher of first authority . . ." (p. 246). In our estimation, however, such recommendations will be easier to implement if commensurate changes also occur in the criteria used for determining access to what the more prestigious colleges have to offer. Otherwise all the customary sources of inducement will remain for using school time below the college level to render the student as proficient as possible at taking tests such as the SAT, and at mastering orthodox academic subject materials in orthodox ways.

If admissions practices at the high selectivity colleges are so influential, how then do they work? The results of our research indicate, first, that they revolve tightly around intelligence test scores and grades; second, that talented attainments of high orders of quality ranging across a wide spectrum of valued fields of human endeavor as exhibited outside the classroom count for relatively little; and third, that such attainments could count for much more, in the sense that favoring students who display them would lead to a class 50 to 60 percent different from the class actually admitted. Why do scores on intelligence tests and academic achievement in high school control the admissions process to the degree that they do? In Chapter 4 we discussed three general factors that seem to be among the elements involved in bringing about this situation. These were the use of score levels on tests such as the SAT as an index by which colleges rank themselves for relative prestige, the increasingly strong role of the faculty in determining admissions decisions, and the growing professionalization of the faculty itself. The latter two factors make for an emphasis on grade-getting ability in college as the major desirable characteristic to be sought among the candidates, and, as we mentioned earlier, intellective aptitude tests and high school grades tend to be the best predictors of college grades—given college curricula as customarily defined. The first factor, in turn, works directly toward an emphasis on intelligence test scores. What we would like to do in this final chapter, however, is to sketch out more fully how these factors make themselves felt in the activities of an admissions committee as it goes about its task of deciding upon acceptances and rejections. Also, we will mention some additional factors that seem to push the admissions process in the same direction.

The intelligence concept—identified as it is at the common-sense level with such other terms as reason and rationality—carries a wide aura of meaning, since it seems to stand for what distinguishes man as a species. Because of his intellectual powers, man has been able to develop the means, within certain limits, to control his own fate and to bend natural events to his will. Transferring this aura of meaning to scores on intelligence tests, and especially to differences among such scores in the upper part of their distributional range is something else again. It is because this transfer takes place that colleges in the first instance are able to view the intelligence test score levels of their students as a means of assessing the national standing of each institution. And the tendency to carry out this transfer of meaning seems to gain reinforcement from the testing agencies, committed as they are to the continued propagation of the tests they manufacture. Testing agencies apart, however, this kind of meaning transfer is not without its functional significance for the faculty —and for the administration as well.

Using scores on tests of intellective ability as a major yardstick according to which collegiate institutions judge themselves, and in terms of which they therefore compete with one another, serves to ease any pressure for curriculum change and other sorts of changes within the college environment itself. This is so because, without changing anything else, admitting more freshmen with higher intelligence test scores will give the college more students who go on to graduate and professional schools, where entrance once again is heavily influenced by scores on intellective aptitude tests. High scorers on the SAT will not only tend to earn higher grades in college, given the customary type of curriculum and grading practices, but will also tend to earn higher scores on the verbal and quantitative aptitude tests of the Graduate Record Examination and on other analogous tests used in the current scheme of things for allocating students to postcollege educational opportunities.

In short, raising the SAT score level of those who enter may well be the easiest way for a college to improve its "academic yield," as defined in terms of conventional educational values. This method does not involve tampering with what is done with and for students during their period of attendance at the college. Such an approach tends to keep the faculty happy, since it minimizes the extent to which they will be pushed by the administration or would feel forced by their own soul-searching into questioning their self-imposed definitions of their academic disciplines and their approaches to teaching. And the administration, of course, would rather not have to push the faculty in such ways. This approach also tends to minimize the number of students on campus who, because they may possess talents in directions not satisfied by the nature of the curricular offerings and emphases, would raise serious challenges to the status quo—challenges that would cause problems for both the faculty and the administration. Such issues, therefore, as whether there should be artists as well as art historians in the art department, whether there should be creative writers as well as literary critics and historians of literature in the English department, whether there should be a degree program in modern dance, whether dramatics should be granted the recognition of having an academic department founded in its behalf or kept in extracurricular limbo, whether playing the harpsichord well is as academically valuable as having a good grasp of the history of baroque music, are not as likely to arise, or will come up only in more muted form.

Each year, as the applications pour in, they must be read and dealt with over a short period of time. While it might well be viewed as theoretically desirable to let the art department go through the applications and pick out a few likely artists, there is not sufficient time or staff to arrange for this, let alone to give all the other departments on campus a turn as well. The exigencies of the moment, coupled with the absence of an admissions plan clearly and explicitly oriented toward admitting particular proportions of applicants with the greatest demonstrated capabilities in the visual arts, in music, in creative writing, in political leadership, and so on, make it hard not to fall back on intellective aptitude test scores and secondary school grades as the basis for accepting or rejecting a candidate. Despite assurances to the contrary by the decision makers, most admissions committee members hang on to the apparent objectivity of intelligence test score and academic achievement credentials. It is understandable that, in the clutch produced by limitations of time and staff, those making the decisions find it difficult to go against the SAT scores and grade records by selecting someone apparently less qualified in these respects—although still possessing respectable academic skills credentials—however remarkably qualified he may be in some other way. It is also understandable that the occasional exception which the committee makes along these lines will tend to receive distortedly heavy emphasis in the minds of the decision makers. This leads them to believe that talented nonacademic attainments outweigh SAT scores and grades in their decisions more often than is the case. The fact remains that keeping an overriding emphasis on SAT scores and grades in the admissions process brings about results that please both the administration and the faculty—an outcome that might not be so readily attainable were decisions to be made on other bases. Since such an emphasis seems, furthermore, to be meritocratic, the alumni cannot strongly object to it.

The attempt to please more than one taskmaster also operates in a rather direct way to keep the admissions process unanalyzed and ambiguous. To some extent, this lack of clarity arises once again from insufficiencies of time and staff. The most important reason for this state of affairs, however, may arise from the problems a college faces in justifying the grounds for admissions decisions to all the interested parties. A justification that would satisfy one reference group would at the same time bring forth a hue and cry from another. To say, for example, that alumni children receive preferential admissions treatment would be acceptable to the alumni but would elicit cries of outrage from the faculty. It is much easier to leave the waters muddy, and even to throw up a considerable smoke screen around the admissions process, leaving the general implication that, by some almost magical means, the "best" applicants are chosen, but otherwise letting the process stay undefined. The upshot of this ambiguity, of course, is that the assumptions guiding the process cannot be readily inspected, subjected to criticism, and compared with possible alternative assumptions that might be made.

It seems to us that one of the reasons why the argument currently rages in public news media as to the desirability or undesirability of "open admissions" is this absence of explicit definition or clarity concerning the bases on which admissions decisions are made. Gaps are suspected to exist between policy statements and actual practices. One or another group of candidates, such as athletes, or those from the geographic region of the institution, or those with the highest SAT scores, are thought to receive special consideration. Those with particular talents, such as in the performing arts, or those from particular backgrounds, are thought to be ignored. But the facts remain murky and mistrust therefore is generated. Colleges have tended not to state frankly and often may well not really know themselves what targets they possess—or if they do possess targets—for numbers of students to be accepted from different geographic regions, or different ethnic groups, or public versus private high schools, or advantaged versus disadvantaged families. The very idea of setting quotas, in fact, has carried with it a strongly pejorative connotation of working against meritocratic values, because quotas sometimes and in some places have been used to restrict the admission of certain minority group members who otherwise, on a meritocratic basis, would have been qualified for admission.

There is nothing malicious or antimeritocratic in principle, however, about the use of certain kinds of quotas. Our research has demonstrated that talent as directly revealed in meritorious real-world accomplishments is diverse rather than unidimensional in the forms that it takes. In order for an admissions policy to reflect this psychological reality, quotas must be established toward the goal of seeking to fill the entering freshman class with certain minimum numbers of persons with strong talents in each of the diverse realms of endeavor where socially and educationally valuable attainments can appropriately be sought. This is a positive use of quotas, the aim of which is to insure that all forms of talented attainments deemed worthy of admissions attention within a meritocratic philosophy end up receiving this consideration. The question is not so much whether meritocratic values will prevail in an admissions approach: by and large, given the nature of the society, some definition of meritocracy will be applied. Rather, the question is whether the means for putting one's meritocratic values into practice will or will not be justifiable and sound in terms of what is known concerning the psychological nature of talent. In other words, will the meritocratic standards used genuinely reflect talent in its real-life manifestations? This is, after all, the ultimate criterion of what the concept should mean.

Our research indicates that admissions practices at a representative high selectivity institution fare poorly in these terms. They tend to pass over large numbers of academically qualified students who have demonstrated intrinsically valuable attainments in one or another field of societal contribution, ranging across various domains of the arts and extending to science and political leadership as well. They favor instead large numbers of students who have somewhat higher academic skills credentials but have not demonstrated attainments of the aforementioned kind. The academic skills differential favoring the latter over the former applicants—a differential between two groups that are both at upper levels in terms of academic qualifications anyway—has no apparent import in terms of environmentally significant accomplishments. The differential that favors the former over the latter applicants when it comes to directly valuable attainments in the real world, on the other hand, speaks for itself as a valid way of making merit distinctions. As discussed in Chapter 1, the attainments are socially valuable in their own right, and also may well offer a good basis for predicting the manifestation of parallel attainments in adult occupational life. Neither of these points can be made in favor of intelligence test score differences and most of what determines secondary school grade differences within this upper sector of the academic skills range.

A clear need exists for acceptance at the level of admissions practices of the proposition that, within the upper part of the academic skills distribution, talent manifests itself in diverse ways not amenable to prediction from intelligence test score and grade achievement distinctions. Were this proposition to become the basis for a changed approach to admissions at the high selectivity colleges, the society would have achieved a direction of admissions reform appropriate for matching and implementing the kind of diversification and broadening of the college curriculum that is espoused with increasing frequency these days as an educationally appropriate goal. Having more students on campus who excel at the types of activities that a liberalized definition of the college curriculum would include, makes curriculum reforms on the one hand more likely in the first place and, on the other, more fruitful and meaningful once they occur.

To award more faculty positions to practitioners in various fields, for example, and to extend academic credit to students for nonlibrary activities and "applied" experiences in those same fields, tends to bring one, as we discussed in Chapter 4, into direct confrontation with the rather entrenched commitments of academic professionalism. Given the relative imperviousness of the academic guild system to criticism from outside the guild itself, these commitments do not change easily or overnight. This resistance to outside pressure is, of course, a strength as well as a weakness of the college and university faculty system. Without enough autonomy and sufficient powers of self-regulation, the faculty would be forever prey to outside interference concerning the proper scope and definition of its activities. These issues should be decided in principle only by those who possess the necessary knowledge and expertise to make meaningful judgments. Without enough responsiveness to the world outside of the classroom, however, scholarly concerns can degenerate into pedantry and faculty autonomy can become a conservative blinder impeding the taking of fresh looks at what should be the appropriate range of inquiry in a field. For that matter, what fields should be deemed worthy of inclusion in the structure of the academy? It has taken the voices of students in recent times to communicate the message that faculty conservatism of the kind just described may often be holding sway. The evidence in the present volume, in turn, serves to point out that such conservatism in effect is aided and abetted by an unjustifiably narrow application of the meritocratic ideal at the admissions end of the picture.

The findings reported in this volume also have pertinence to the controversy that has swirled around Jensen's proposal (1969) that heredity is more important than environment in causing the superior performance of whites over blacks on intelligence tests and on scholastic achievement. Both Jensen *and* his critics (Harvard Educational Review, 1969) appear to share in some degree the implicit assumption that intelligence test scores and their academic achievement correlate are of overwhelming importance across the full distributional range as indicating the likelihood of a person's exhibiting intrinsically meritorious talented accomplishments. To the degree that this assumption turns out to be invalid, the need for waging the controversy diminishes, for IQ scores and grade achievement differences will have less societal significance than was thought—however hereditary or environmental may be their basis.

What we have found, of course, suggests that a positive relationship between intelligence test scores and grade quality, on the one hand, and direct criteria of talented attainments, on the other, is not present within the upper sector of the academic skills distribution. Rather, for that part of the academic skills range, further increments on measures of academic aptitude and achievement do not seem to possess clear significance for environmentally demonstrated attainments reflecting some form of talent. Yet we have also found that intelligence test score and grade achievement increments within that same upper part of the range for academic skills exert a strong determining influence over college admissions practices. Just as there seems to be no reason for paying attention to intellective aptitude test score differences and grade quality differences within this upper sector when it comes to making preferential selections for access to the more prestigious colleges, there also seems to be no reason for serious concern over whether these same differences are to be accounted for in terms of heredity or environment. While, to be sure, this point in no sense eliminates the basis for the controversy between Jensen and his critics, it does suggest some limitations on the degree of psychological import and therefore of social significance possessed by the controversy. In brief, to the extent that intelligence test scores and grades have less meaning than was assumed, then to that extent less hinges upon how the controversy between Jensen and his critics is resolved.

Where do we go from here? It has not been our intention, of course, to write a cookbook for admissions reform. What we *have* done is provide evidence that current admissions practices at high selectivity institutions emphasize intellective aptitude test score differences and secondary school grade record differences to a greater degree than is justifiable. At the same time they fail to provide a sufficient degree of emphasis on direct indications of talented attainments reflecting the actual real-world competences of those who apply. We have discussed why this state of affairs seems to have come about and why it is important, both in terms of individuals and in terms of the society as a whole, to remedy this situation. The empirical documenting of these points required that we utilize assessment procedures that would specify in public terms what we meant by such concepts as excellence in the dramatic arts or significant talent at creative writing. It also required that we work out a means of making decisions on the basis of such procedures. Therefore, the approach that we have followed can be duplicated by anyone who wishes to use it in an actual admissions setting. We do not intend it, however, to function as a final pronouncement on exactly how change should take place. Rather, it illustrates the *type* of reform that, on the basis of the evidence that we have gathered, seems to be desirable. And it illustrates as well that change of this kind is within the realm of practicality.

Such change will not, of course, be completely without problems. If evidence of writing or sculpturing ability or carrying out scientific projects receives greater weight than heretofore as a basis for admission to the more prestigious institutions, some applicants may, for example, try to write something that gets published in a nationally circulated periodical not because they are interested in writing but because they want to better their chance for college admission. We do not worry seriously about this kind of issue, however, for two reasons. First, there will always be pressures upon students to do whatever will increase their admissions access to high selectivity colleges. Given those circumstances, it seems more reasonable for pressures of that kind to be directed toward the full panoply of ways in which talent genuinely manifests itself, rather than toward a narrow and interrelated set of skills— doing as well as possible at intellective aptitude tests and at the usual kinds of secondary school courses—that can be cultivated and displayed without that much meaning for real-life attainments. With college entrance pressures oriented toward more veridical definitions of merit, students will be encouraged thereby to spend more time and effort doing whatever they are really best at anyway, because excellence at that very activity—at least across a wide and diversified range of possibilities—will be viewed as a legitimate basis for appraisal.

The second reason has to do with what Allport (1961) has called "functional autonomy." If a high school student starts out writing poetry for publication in a well-known literary magazine with the idea of its helping him gain admission to a college he would like to attend (and if his poetry is good enough to be published), then the fact is that he has written poetry which is thought by presumably competent judges to be of superior quality. However extrinsic or instrumental may have been the initial push to do it—and motivational patterns are more often complex than simple—some good poetry has resulted. If he now proceeds to write poetry often enough and well enough, what may have begun as an extrinsically motivated activity may end up as an activity carried out for its own sake. In any case, he has discovered that he is capable of writing poetry that interests other people, and he has given the world some poetry of quality which it did not have before. If college admissions criteria have the effect of inducing students to carry out inherently worthwhile activities which they may not have done otherwise, this is hardly an outcome to complain about. And it may just happen that the new experience which is thereby generated comes to be valued for its own sake.

No doubt the particular sources of evidence to be depended on as reflections of intrinsically meritorious attainments in one or another line of endeavor can be reviewed and modified. No doubt as well, there are additional domains in which one might seek demonstrations of talent—such as, for example, modern dance. The essential point made by our work, however, is that admissions decisions can profitably focus upon attainments that are of direct value in their own right, upon evidence of what the person has in fact done which the real world views as significant, rather than so heavily upon scores and indicators that turn out not to possess the kind of broad environmental significance that is imputed to them. To bring about this shift in focus, college admissions decisions should be geared toward filling the entering class with subgroups representing different kinds of directly meaningful talented attainments. Through the combined use of environmentally defined talented accomplishments as evidences of merit, and a decision-making approach that insures the representation of diverse kinds of talent, the college admissions process should be able to play a maximally constructive role in the nourishment of this society's human potential.

References

Ackerman, J. S. Two styles: A challenge to higher education. *Daedalus*, 1969, *98*, 855–869.

Allport, G. W. *Pattern and growth in personality*. New York: Holt, Rinehart and Winston, 1961.

Astin, A. W. *Who goes where to college?* Chicago: Science Research Associates, 1965.

Ausubel, D. P. *Educational psychology: A cognitive view*. New York: Holt, Rinehart and Winston, 1968.

Bloom, B. S. Report on creativity research by the examiner's office of the University of Chicago. In C. W. Taylor and F. Barron (Eds.), *Scientific creativity: Its recognition and development*. New York: Wiley, 1963. Pp. 251–264.

Bruner, J. S. *The process of education*. Cambridge, Mass.: Harvard University Press, 1960.

Bruner, J. S. *Toward a theory of instruction*. Cambridge, Mass.: Harvard University Press, 1966.

College Entrance Examination Board. *Manual of freshman class profiles*, 1965–1967. New York: College Entrance Examination Board, 1965.

College Entrance Examination Board. *College Board score reports: A guide for counselors and admissions officers*. New York: College Entrance Examination Board, 1968.

Davis, J. A. The campus as a frog pond: An application of the theory of relative deprivation to career decisions of college men. *American Journal of Sociology*, 1966, *72*, 17–30.

Fishman, J. A. Some social-psychological theory for selecting and guiding college students. In N. Sanford (Ed.), *The American college.* New York: Wiley, 1962. Pp. 666–689.

Friedenberg, E. Z. The university community in an open society. *Daedalus,* 1970, *99,* 56–74.

Gardner, J. W. *Excellence.* New York: Harper & Row, 1961.

Glimp, F. L. Student diversity and national goals in higher education. In, *The economics of higher education.* New York: College Entrance Examination Board, 1967. Pp. 18–28.

Goslin, D. A. What's wrong with tests and testing—Part I. *College Board Review,* 1967 (Fall), 12–18.

Harmon, L. R. The development of a criterion of scientific competence. In C. W. Taylor and F. Barron (Eds.), *Scientific creativity: Its recognition and development.* New York: Wiley, 1963. Pp. 44–52.

Harvard Educational Review. *Environment, heredity, and intelligence: Reprint series no. 2, compiled from the Harvard Educational Review.* Cambridge, Mass.: Harvard Educational Review, 1969.

Hays, W. L. *Statistics for psychologists.* New York: Holt, Rinehart and Winston, 1963.

Heist, P. (Ed.) *The creative college student: An unmet challenge.* San Francisco: Jossey-Bass, 1968.

Holland, J. L. Creative and academic performance among talented adolescents. *Journal of Educational Psychology,* 1961, *52,* 136–147.

Holland, J. L., and Astin, A. W. The prediction of the academic, artistic, scientific, and social achievement of undergraduates of superior scholastic aptitude. *Journal of Educational Psychology,* 1962, *53,* 132–143.

Holland, J. L., and Nichols, R. C. Prediction of academic and extracurricular achievement in college. *Journal of Educational Psychology,* 1964, *55,* 55–65.

Holland, J. L., and Richards, J. M., Jr. Academic and nonacademic accomplishment: Correlated or uncorrelated? *Journal of Educational Psychology,* 1965, *56,* 165–174.

Holland, J. L., and Richards, J. M., Jr. The many faces of talent: A reply to Werts. *Journal of Educational Psychology,* 1967, *58,* 205–209.

Holt, J. *The underachieving school.* New York: Pitman, 1969.

Hoyt, D. P. The relationship between college grades and adult achievement: A review of the literature. *American College Testing Program Research Reports,* 1965, No. 7.

Hoyt, D. P. College grades and adult accomplishment: A review of research. *The Educational Record,* 1966 (Winter), 70–75.

Hoyt, D. P. Forecasting academic success in specific colleges. *American College Testing Program Research Reports,* 1968, No. 27.

Jencks, C., and Riesman, D. *The academic revolution.* Garden City, N.Y.: Doubleday, 1968.

Jensen, A. R. How much can we boost IQ and scholastic achievement? In, Harvard Educational Review. *Environment, heredity, and intelligence: Reprint series no. 2, compiled from the Harvard Educational Review.* Cambridge, Mass.: Harvard Educational Review, 1969. Pp. 1–123.

Jones, R. M. *Fantasy and feeling in education.* New York: New York University Press, 1968.

MacKinnon, D. W. Selecting students with creative potential. In P. Heist (Ed.), *The creative college student: An unmet challenge.* San Francisco: Jossey-Bass, 1968. Pp. 101–116.

Mayer, M. *The schools.* New York: Harper & Row, 1961.

McClelland, D. C. Issues in the identification of talent. In D. C. McClelland, A. L. Baldwin, U. Bronfenbrenner, and F. L. Strodtbeck, *Talent and society: New perspectives in the identification of talent.* Princeton, N.J.: Van Nostrand, 1958. Pp. 1–28.

Richards, J. M., Jr., Holland, J. L., and Lutz, Sandra W. Prediction of student accomplishment in college. *Journal of Educational Psychology,* 1967, *58,* 343–355.

Stein, M. I. *Personality measures in admissions: Antecedent and personality factors as predictors of college success.* New York: College Entrance Examination Board, 1963.

Thresher, B. A. *College admissions and the public interest.* New York: College Entrance Examination Board, 1966.

Tyler, Leona E. *The psychology of human differences.* (Third edit.) New York: Appleton-Century-Crofts, 1965.

Wallach, M. A., and Kogan, N. *Modes of thinking in young children: A study of the creativity-intelligence distinction.* New York: Holt, Rinehart and Winston, 1965.

Wallach, M. A., and Wing, C. W., Jr. *The talented student: A validation of the creativity-intelligence distinction.* New York: Holt, Rinehart and Winston, 1969.

Whitla, D. K. Evaluation of decision making: A study of college admissions. In D. K. Whitla (Ed.), *Handbook of measurement and assessment in behavioral sciences.* Reading, Mass.: Addison-Wesley, 1968. Pp. 456–490.

Wolfle, D. Diversity of talent. *American Psychologist,* 1960, *15,* 535–545.

INDEX